Alexandra Fraser is a company director of Maverick TV and produced the popular *Trade Secrets* television programme. Katherine Lapworth is a self-employed copywriter. They met when they worked at the BBC and have written together for the last few years, including the first *Trade Secrets* books. They are well qualified to write this book as they both have mothers who are shining examples of the species. As a dutiful daughter, Katherine got her mother to proofread the book and test drive as many of the tips as possible. Alexandra took research into motherhood a little further and produced Harry, Paddy and Anna. So far, all three children are thriving, so she must be doing something right.

GW00729159

Trade Secrets
MOTHER'S
DAY

Alexandra Fraser
and Katherine Lapworth

ORION

An Orion paperback

First published in Great Britain in 2005
by Orion
Orion House, 5 Upper St Martin's Lane,
London WC2H 9EA

A CIP catalogue record for this book is available
from the British Library.

ISBN 0 75286 419 X

Printed by LegoPrint, Italy

www.orionbooks.co.uk

Contents

Introduction

Even the Old Woman Who Lived in a Shoe needed a bit of quiet, quality time to herself, away from all those children. Whether you are a new mum (wearing the badge of regurgitated milk on your shoulder), grappling with truculent teenagers or are a hardened survivor whose brood has now left home, you are not 'just a mum' but still a lovely woman who deserves to have a bit of time and effort dedicated simply to you.

Let's face it, most mothers spread themselves pretty thin when it comes to family, obligations, timetables, career, chores . . . The last person to be looked after on a mother's list is, well, the mother herself. This book is all about making life easier and pampering yourself, too. It won't take pots of money, just a bit of canny know-how and the ability to put yourself first now and again. Oh, yes, and to remember that you are a gorgeous woman.

So what better time to start pampering yourself than on Mother's Day?

'There is no pleasure in having nothing to do . . . the fun is having lots to do and not doing it.' *Mary Little*

Trade Secrets
MOTHER'S DAY

Pamper, Cosset and Indulge

No, that isn't the name of a firm of solicitors (although it might be a good one for a sweet shop). This is all about making time for yourself. Having a few moments – you are a busy woman after all – to pamper, cosset and indulge yourself. Having recharged your batteries, you can take whatever the world (and your children) throw at you!

'I love people. I love my family, my children ... but inside myself is a place where I live all alone and that's where you renew your springs that never dry up.' *Pearl S. Buck*

Wear some luxurious underwear – even if it's a 'jeans and sweatshirt' day. It's wonderful to have an indulgent secret.

Turn off your mobile and put the answer machine on – at least once a week. Have some quiet time for yourself.

Make even the most mundane chores a bit special – treat yourself to a glass of wine in a crystal glass. Stand it on a beautifully decorated tray.

Wake up to the smell of fresh bread. Invest in a bread-making machine with a timer. Then, you can gradually come to with the smell of fresh bread wafting through the house. In your half-awake, half-asleep state, imagine you are in some chic little hotel in Paris. Then, wake up properly, go downstairs and enjoy buttery toast and a cup of coffee.

Tear out sample perfume strips from women's magazines and store them in your underwear drawers (car, handbag or wardrobe). Change them regularly to keep smells fresh.

Go and see a film ... with a girlfriend. Ideally, if you can, go to a matinee showing, buy a box of chocolates and escape to Tinseltown for a couple of hours.

Be uplifted. Put postcards, photos or pictures from your favourite magazines on the inside of your wardrobe or inside your kitchen cupboard doors. Every time you open the door, you'll see something you love.

Look through your old photograph albums. That will always raise a smile.

Keep a wish-list file or box – things you want to do (however fantastic), where you want to go (no matter how far away), the kind of home you want to live in (castle in Spain? villa in France?). You can be as realistic or as over the top as you want. Then whenever you want a boost, rifle through the file and see things that give you pleasure.

Compile a list of your favourite music. Put together a tape or CD. Play it in the car or when you're doing the housework.

Make a list of ten things you would like to do before next Mother's Day.

Treat yourself to a glossy magazine. Whether it's about fashion, home and garden or general lifestyle, see how the other half live . . . and dream a little.

Write a letter to a friend. Not an email, not a scribbled postcard, but a letter. Preferably on smart, thick writing paper. Spend a bit of quiet, quality time telling them what you and the family have been up to. You will enjoy doing it, your friend will be delighted and appreciate the thought and, like casting bread upon the waters, you could soon see exciting envelopes (not the brown 'bills' variety) dropping on to your doormat.

Lower your stress levels by eating an orange.

Invite your friends over for a themed dinner or tea party.

Have a pedicure – if your feet feel fine then so does the rest of you.

Light a fire and curl up in front of it. To get the most from your fire, put a couple of drops of pine, sandalwood or cedarwood oil on to the wood that you are going to burn. Leave it for an hour before lighting the fire. As the fire burns, the fragrance is released into the room.

Give your fridge a facelift – pop in a small

bunch of flowers to brighten your day every time you open the fridge door.

Throw out your old tea towels and treat yourselves – and your kitchen – to a new look.

Create your own tea ceremony. Next time you stop for a cup of tea in the afternoon, make it a bit of an occasion. Have a few small sandwiches (egg, cucumber) and some tiny cakes.

Take riding lessons – great exercise (firms the thighs), great outfits and a great challenge!

Buy yourself a bag of sweets to remind you of your childhood – good for emergencies when you need to cheer yourself up.

Indulge your alter ego – put some thought into your username for your email account. mum@ourhouse.com is a bit mundane. In fact, you could have several to suit your mood. Never mind mother, wife, daughter . . . how about QueenoftheUniverse, PrincessMagnificent and SheWhoMustBeObeyed@ourhouse.com?

'There are two things to aim at in life: first get what you want; and after that to enjoy it.' *Logan Persall Smith*

Farewell to Fatigue

Running a house? Running a family? Running a business? Running all three? Time to wind down and relax. Give yourself and your body a break. We all need to recharge our batteries at some point. Make sure that you get the most from your periods of rest and recuperation.

'People who say they sleep like a baby usually don't have one.' *Leo Burke*

We can't all drape ourselves in cashmere from head to food. But a little goes a long way. Wear cashmere socks to bed – it's the best way to fall asleep quickly.

A four-poster bed is the ultimate luxury. Put up curtain tracks or poles on the ceiling, lined up with the sides of the bed, and hang curtains from them. Tie them back during the day for a real boudoir feel. Who knows, Prince Charming may even kiss you awake! Alternatively, hang a panel of beautiful material (or sumptuous wallpaper) behind the bed. This draws the eye, making the bed the focal point of the room and giving the impression of height and space.

Banish those comfy old slippers and get some kitten-heeled mules to wear instead (OK, you can keep the old slippers for when you're having 'fat days' but hide them away). Instant glamour and you'll feel like a movie star. Lana Turner, eat your heart out!

'Sex is essentially just a matter of good lighting.' *Noël Coward*

For a restful, warm, welcoming glow in the bedroom, use tinted 40- or 60-watt light bulbs rather than the harsh 100-watt white bulbs.

For a relaxing read before bedtime, make sure your bedside light shades are just above your head when lying down. Then they will be high enough to throw light on to the page but not on to your face.

To stimulate and soothe your whole body, get your feet wet! Put 5 drops of lavender oil into a hot foot bath and give your feet a soak. The soles of your feet are very porous and can absorb the lavender oil quickly into the bloodstream.

A cup of camomile tea before bed will help you sleep.

For a relaxing night's sleep, use scented candles, pot pourri and linen spray – although not necessarily all at the same time if you want to avoid sensory overload. Lavender, camomile and rosemary are all good for this. Make sure the 'smells' are relaxing and not sickly sweet and cloying. Keep a mix of different kinds of smells so you can reflect your different moods.

Burning essential oils can create an oasis of calm as well. Put a metal ring on a light bulb with a few drops of oil on the ring. As the light from the bulb heats up the ring, the oils are released.

Give pot pourri a bit of a stir every time you go past the bowl. This keeps it looking fresh and gives out a waft of its scent at the same time.

Incense sticks are another way to create a lovely smell but, like the pot pourri, don't economise. Buy the best you can afford, otherwise everything ends up smelling of stale smoke and ancient hippies.

To wind down, put a few drops of essential oils (such as lavender, mandarin, marjoram and petitgrain) in your bath and on your pillow.

Also, at bedtime, you can put a couple of drops of lavender oil on your pillow to relax you. Ylang ylang is an alternative choice – it's a great aphrodisiac.

Surround yourself with uplifting or relaxing fragrances, use essential oils to create the mood. To make your own inexpensive room spray, add 10 drops of your favourite essential oil to a plant spray or vaporiser filled with 7 tablespoons of warm water. One tablespoon of vodka or pure alcohol acts as a preservative.

When using essential oils in a vaporiser, use 2 to 3 drops for a small room and 6 to 10 drops for a larger room.

If you don't have a vaporiser, put 5 drops of essential oil in a small bowl of water and place it on a radiator.

Don't overdo it. Avoid essential oils for 48 hours every week.

Make wonderful scented drawer liners by adding a couple of drops of essential oil to some pretty wrapping paper. Alternatively, when you have finished a bottle of perfume, don't throw it away. Take the top off and put the bottle in among your clothes.

Put a couple of drops of your favourite oil on your handkerchief. A great idea, especially if you've got a cold.

Large amounts of clary sage oil can cause drowsiness, so don't use it before driving or operating machinery.

Avoid clary sage if you are on hormone replacement therapy (HRT).

Avoid peppermint oil close to bedtime because it can cause insomnia.

For a late-night snack to help you sleep, try cottage cheese and dates. They contain tryptophan, an amino acid that encourages sleep.

'If you think women are the weaker sex, try pulling the blankets back to your side.'
Stuart Turner

The bedroom needn't be just for sleeping. Make it your special haven from the rest of the world (and the family) – put a comfy chair in one corner and curl up with a good book and a hot chocolate from time to time.

Create a bit of bedroom luxury, use cushions and throws in touchy-feely fabrics (such as satins, furs and velvets).

How old is your mattress? If it's 10 years or older, creaks and groans when you move about on it (the mattress, not your other half) and you find you roll into the middle of the bed, then it's time to say goodbye to it and get a new one.

If the mattress is fine but you fancy a new look, get a new headboard. You could make your own using plywood cut to size. Cover it with wadding and then with the fabric of your choice.

Wet, Wet, Wet

After the bedroom, the other essential haven in the house for mums is the bathroom. Now we're not talking about the early morning shower, in and out of the bathroom in minutes and off to work, or the water fight with the children before bedtime. This is all about winding down and tickling your senses . . . not about getting clean!

'Give me the luxuries in life and I will willingly do without the necessities.' *Frank Lloyd Wright*

Make your own luxury bath oil. Get some baby oil and put a few drops of your favourite perfume into it, give the mix a swirl and then pour into a hot bath (don't put the perfume straight into the hot water – as it will just dissolve into nothing). You get to relax and unwind and the bathroom ends up smelling fabulous.

Keep the door closed so that the vapours don't escape and the family can't get in to disturb you.

Drop fresh flower heads on to the water for a finishing touch.

Milk baths soften skin – add 1 pint/600 ml of milk to your bath water and pretend you are Cleopatra.

For baby-smooth skin, add a cupful of milk granules to your bath and enjoy a long soak.

If you don't have heated towel rails, put your towels in the tumble dryer while you bathe or shower so that when you emerge, like Venus from the water, you can wrap yourself in warm towels.

If you have sensitive skin, mix the essential oil with a base oil, such as sweet almond or apricot oil, before pouring into the bath.

Oils are lovely in a bath but can make things slippery. To avoid slip-sliding away, mix the oil with some full-fat milk or dairy cream before adding it to the water.

Always wipe the bath down after use. Some essential oils can mark plastic baths if they are left on the surface.

After peeling an avocado, rub the inside of the skin over your knees and elbows – or anywhere else that needs softening.

A handful of dry sea salt rubbed over the body before a bath helps to slough off dead skin.

Oatmeal makes a good alternative to soap – put a handful in a muslin bag and use it in the bath as a body scrub.

Salt baths help to heal any wounds or scratches on the skin. Add a cup of salt to the bath water.

Dry skin? Add a drop or two of good-quality olive oil to your bath.

Don't throw old fruit away. Pop any fruit that's gone too soft into the blender. Use the mixture as an all-over body mask and nutrient. Once you shower it off, your skin will feel really soft and you'll smell good enough to eat.

If you suffer from bad circulation, try alternating hot and cold showers to get your system moving.

'By and large, mothers and housewives are the only workers who do not have regular time off. They are the great vacation-less class.' *Anne Morrow Lingbergh*

Bathtime treats

To give yourself a good back scrub, place a bar of soap inside the middle of a stocking or chopped-off tights leg. Knot the stocking on each side of the soap. Hold one end of the stocking in each hand and, with a see-sawing motion, scrub your back.

For a wonderful foot bath, quarter-fill a washing-up bowl with warm water and add 5 drops of your favourite essential oil diluted in a cup of vodka (or pure alcohol).

For a bathtime treat, make your own herbal infusion. Put dried herbs in a muslin bag (you can use fresh herbs but these are not as concentrated as dried ones), tie it to the hot-water tap so that the water flows over and through the bag. When the bath is ready, put the bag in the water and leave it to float around while you bathe.

For a reviving bath, use herbs such as mint, thyme, nettles (to boost circulation) and pine (which is refreshing).

For a relaxing bath, use lavender, marjoram (a great natural tranquilliser), sage (an anti-dote for stress) and lemon balm (which relieves tension).

OK, just a brief nod to that early morning dash to get out of the house . . . for a quick boost of energy, run your wrists under cold water.

Finish off your morning shower with a blast of cold water for a couple of minutes. Wakes you up a treat and gets your circulation going.

Mmmm, massage

'When my children are unruly, I use a nice safe play pen. When they're finished, I climb out.' *Erma Bombeck*

When giving – or more importantly, being given – a massage, make sure that the room is warm and that there is a suitable, comfortable area to work in.

Make sure there are no distractions: take the phone off the hook and send the children round to friends.

Warm hands – good. Cold hands – a big shock. Always make sure your masseuse's hands are warm before being given a massage!

Candles give a wonderful light and create just the right sort of atmosphere. Avoid harsh overhead lighting when giving a massage.

You will need lots of towels. Towels to lie on, to drape over you, to rest your head, feet or back on. Warm them up in the airing cupboard

or a tumble dryer just before you start.

Develop your sense of smell. Start with just 4 essential oils. Find a quiet, undisturbed place and take time to get to know and recognise these smells. Sniff each one separately; see what emotions, memories and feelings they evoke. You will find you respond to certain smells more than others. Use them to help you create the desired mood.

Oils should be stored away from direct sunlight, in the cool and dark. They will last for about a year if stored properly.

Citrus oils don't last for very long, so only buy small amounts at any one time.

To preserve the label, paint with clear nail varnish. This works for medicine bottles too.

'Women and cats will do as they please, and men and dogs should relax and get used to the idea.' *Robert A. Heinlein*

Never buy cheap oils because they just don't do the job. The more expensive ones are more effective.

To keep oil fresh, never put new oil in an old bottle.

When an oil has gone bad, it will appear cloudy and give off an unpleasant smell. Essential oils should be clear.

Carrier oils are used to dilute the essential oil. They allow the essential oil to be spread over the body and to be absorbed into the skin properly. They are ideal for dry or sensitive skins. Cold-pressed oils are the best. Sweet almond oil is most commonly used: it's non-allergenic, neutral and can be used for massaging babies.

Choose the right carrier oil. Sesame oil is great for stretch marks, walnut balances the nervous system, apricot and peach kernel – as well as evening primrose oil – are best for cell regeneration. For menstrual problems, use walnut or evening primrose oil.

To make your carrier oils go further, add 5 to 10 per cent of wheatgerm oil, which helps to preserve the mixture.

To mix your essential oils with the carrier oil, use a toothpick.

Never put an undiluted essential oil directly on to your skin – except for one drop of tea tree or lavender oil.

To increase the life of the scent from your oils, add some sandalwood oil, which acts as a fixative.

Always do a patch test before applying oils to check that you, or whoever you are intending to use the oils on, are not allergic to any of them.

To mix enough oil for a body massage, mix 10 drops of essential oil with 2 teaspoons

of carrier oil. You will need more carrier oil
for a person with a lot of body hair.

Looking Good

'So much has been said and sung of beautiful
young girls, why don't somebody wake up to
the beauty of old women.' So said Harriet
Beecher Stowe and 'Absolutely' say we. Well,
'old' is a relative term but whatever your age,
you can still look glowing and gorgeous.

**'Sex appeal is fifty per cent what you've
got** and fifty per cent what people think
you've got.' *Sophia Loren*

**Retain your youthful features – eat more
avocados.** They contain monounsaturated
acids that lower cholesterol and are packed
full of vitamin E, which is believed to slow
the ageing process.

Kick-start your digestion each morning by
drinking some warm water with lemon juice
squeezed into it.

A good way to boost circulation and get
your lymph system going is to sit in a warm
bath with your feet in a bowl of cold water.
OK, slight gymnastics involved here but it's
worth it for the jump-start it gives your
system. If you can swap round and plonk
your bottom in the cold water and your feet
in the warm, well, so much the better!

If you are feeling sluggish, eat a banana or

a pear – they help to cleanse the liver and get rid of toxins.

Moody because of poor digestion? Eat a kiwi fruit – it's high in vitamins C, E and potassium.

Have a mini-detox. Eat an apple and some yogurt.

Eat eggs to clear up a cold – they're high in zinc, which helps cure colds.

Talking can make you thinner! If you stand during a 15-minute chat on the phone, you will burn 25 calories. Sitting down only uses up 10.

Can't be bothered with the gym? Then go walkabout. Walking briskly can use up 500 calories an hour. Just 5 minutes can lower blood pressure and cholesterol levels, increase bone density, boost your brain power and blow the cobwebs away – and it doesn't cost a penny.

Want a flatter stomach? Try pulling in your tummy muscles every time you walk through a door.

For a pert bottom, squeeze your buttock muscles and hold for about a minute. Why not set a reminder to do this as your screen-saver?

To firm up your bum, carefully walk up the stairs backwards.

To improve the fronts of your thighs and your bum muscles, walk up the stairs two at a time.

You don't need to buy expensive dumb-bells for a basic workout – use large plastic bottles of water.

You can make your own cheap weights by using baked-bean cans.

If you don't have an exercise bike, sit on an ordinary cycle propped up against a wall and cycle backwards.

'Success is the key to happiness. Happiness is the key to success. If you love what you are doing, you will be successful.' *Albert Schweitzer*

Don't weigh yourself when training. You'll get despondent because muscle weighs more than fat and you'll think you're getting fatter! Measure yourself instead and you'll realise the good you're achieving as your body changes shape.

If you are running out of steam, it is psychologically easier to count backwards when exercising. So . . . 5, 4, 3, 2, 1!

To strengthen your thighs, sit against a wall without a chair and build up the time you can hold this position. Always remember to stretch out before and after the exercise.

If you want to lose weight from your

hips, avoid spicy foods because they over-stimulate the glands that cause fat storage in your hips and bum.

Eat vegetable soup as a starter to lose weight. The fibre causes the rest of the meal to pass through your digestive system more quickly.

Also to reduce the amount you eat use smaller dishes. Large plates make you want to eat as much as you can fit on to them. It's all psychological.

Skin Deep

'I'm tired of all this nonsense about beauty being only skin deep. That's deep enough. What do you want, an adorable pancreas?' *Jean Kerr*

Give tired skin a boost – use a honey facial. Apply honey to clean skin, leave on for one hour, then rinse off with warm water.

Cucumber and yogurt make a great face mask. Blend some mashed cucumber with natural yogurt and apply to your face. Leave for about 15 minutes, then rinse off with warm water. Cucumber cools and tones while yogurt acts as a pick-me-up for tired skin.

Get a healthy glow. Dip a cotton pad in some rose water and glycerin and then buff the skin of your face and forehead. Alternatively, mix a teaspoon of double cream, a teaspoon of chick-pea flour, 2 teaspoons water and a pinch of salt and, wait for it, don't eat it – put it on your face. Leave for 10 minutes and then wipe off with damp cotton wool pads.

Before putting on any face mask, cover your skin with a thin layer of gauze and apply the mask over it. You'll get the benefits of the ingredients seeping through and, when it's time to take the mask off, you can simply peel the gauze away. It's much quicker and you don't damage your skin by scrubbing at stubborn bits of the mask.

Open your pores by putting your face over a bowl of hot steamy water. Cover your head with a towel to keep the steam in. If you've got oily skin, stay there for at least 5 minutes.

Don't waste money on expensive facial water sprays – just use a regular plant spray bottle filled with some mineral water. It's great for hot days and sets make-up a treat.

Make sure you take your make-up off even when you come in really late after partying the night away. Have a small plastic storage box of ready-dampened cotton wool pads by your bed to make the task as easy and quick as possible.

There's no need to buy expensive make-up removers – baby oil does the job brilliantly.

Cold milk removes make-up, too.

Or you could try petroleum jelly.
It removes eye make-up, lipstick and blusher just as effectively.

Save your expensive toner – apply it using wet cotton wool. If you use dry, the cotton wool absorbs most of the toner and your skin doesn't get the benefit.

For a cheap moisturiser, blend a banana with a little milk, smooth on to your face and leave for 20 minutes.

If the weather's very hot and you have a tendency to become 'shiny', make it look deliberate! Wear lip gloss and sheen on your eyelids.

Loose powder often looks too heavy because it sticks to moisturisers and cleansers. Blot your face with a tissue before you put any powder on.

Apply loose powder with throwaway cotton-wool pads. The puff provided with the powder will quickly build up dirt and won't do your skin any favours.

If you've got a reddish complexion, use a foundation with a greenish tinge. Applied under normal make-up, this will help to neutralise the red.

If you've got the odd pimple, wipe it gently with a cotton pad soaked in lemon juice.

A great way to dry up any pimples is to smear toothpaste on them.

To get rid of spots, mix 3 teaspoons of honey with one teaspoon of cinnamon and dab the mixture on to your face nightly. In 2 weeks you'll have really clear skin.

Face flannels can be thoroughly sterilised by 'cooking' them damp in a microwave oven for 5 minutes.

Remove dead skin and beat facial blackheads by adding a teaspoon of sugar to your soap.

If you've got a really, really bad spot, you'll never be able to cover it up. Instead, turn it into a trendy beauty spot with a dark eyeliner pencil.

'A woman has the age she deserves.' *Coco Chanel*

Eye, Eye

If your eyes are tired, cup your palms over them and rest your elbows on a table. Take slow, deep, relaxing breaths for a few minutes.

Get rid of under-eye puffiness. Grate some raw potato and apply to the area.

If you use eye cream, keep it in the fridge so it's always refreshingly cool when you apply it.

Give extra sparkle to your eyes. Using a white make-up pencil, draw a line across the lower rim of your eyelid.

When applying mascara, look down directly into a mirror. It makes it impossible to get mascara into the eyes.

When you run out of mascara, stand the tube in a cup of hot water for a minute. This will loosen the last bit of mascara and allow you to use it for at least two more coats.

Eyeliners need to be really sharp. Try chilling eye pencils in the fridge before sharpening them to get a really pointy point.

Avoid smudgy eyeliner by dipping a wet brush in dark eye shadow and using this to line the eyes instead. It will stay on all day.

Run out of eye make-up remover? Use petroleum jelly or Vaseline instead. This even works for waterproof mascara.

Make your own eye make-up remover using one part baby shampoo to 20 parts boiled, cooled water.

If your eyelids are sticky in the morning, dip a cotton bud in baby shampoo (which doesn't sting) and use it to clean the roots of your lashes. Then wash your eyes in clear, cool water.

When using eye cream at night, never put

it too close to your eyes or they'll look puffy
in the morning.

If you do suffer from puffy eyes first thing
in the morning, simply lie down again for 5
minutes with used tea bags over your eyes.

If your eyes are puffy after washing, apply
the pulp of a roasted apple to your eyelids.

'Men don't know anything about pain;
they have never experienced labour, cramps
or a bikini wax.' *Nan Tisdale*

Lip-smacking Lovely

Wearing white? Leave that bright red lipstick at home. Natural make-up in neutral
colours looks best.

**To get the deepest, longest-lasting effect
from lipstick,** powder your lips before applying the lipstick.

To mend a broken lipstick, carefully melt
the broken edges with a lighted match and
press them together. Smooth down the join
with a toothpick and then leave the lipstick
in the fridge for a couple of hours.

Hand-y Hints

For heavy-duty hand cream, mix virgin
olive oil and petroleum jelly together. Rub the
mixture into your hands and then put freezer
bags over your hands. Sit down and relax

with a cuppa or read the paper while your hands absorb this perfect conditioner.

To exfoliate and soften hands, work a mixture of olive oil and granulated sugar into them, then rinse off.

If you have excess moisturiser on your hands, don't rinse it off. Run your fingers through your hair – the cream will prevent frizz and makes a great conditioner.

Clean grubby nails – especially if you're a smoker – with minty toothpaste.

For a soothing hand lotion, soak marigold petals in almond oil for a couple of weeks.

Push back cuticles with lollipop sticks.

When filing nails, keep going in one direction. Sawing backwards and forwards weakens the edges.

Keep nail varnish in the fridge – it lasts for much longer and dries much more quickly when applied.

Stop the top of the nail-varnish bottle from sticking – rub some petroleum jelly on to the top of the bottle.

Avoid bubbles in your nail varnish by gently rolling the bottle to mix it, rather than shaking it (as we all do).

Remove any stains left by nail varnish by

dipping your nails into fresh lemon juice.

Best Foot Forward

Barefoot is best – give your feet a rest each day and walk about the house with no shoes on.

Give your feet a treat. Cover them with a moisturising face mask (yes, face mask), and relax for 10 minutes. Then wipe off the excess, cleanse with toner and rub a little oil into the cuticles.

If you've been on your feet all day, give them a rest and a bit of a pampering session. A cup of baking soda or Epsom salts dissolved in a bowl of warm water makes a wonderful foot bath.

If you want to avoid aching feet, lie or sit down with your feet higher than your hips for at least 15 minutes.

Sprinkle some talc inside your socks or shoes to keep feet dry and smelling sweet.

Strengthen your ankles while watching television. Keep moving them in a circular motion.

To cure anhydrosis (dry skin on the soles of your feet to you or me), try rubbing petroleum jelly into your feet every night without fail. Wear towelling socks overnight. The dry skin will soon disappear.

Smelly feet? Try rubbing in a little eucalyptus oil.

After having your legs waxed allow them to breathe. If you put tight trousers or stockings back on immediately you are encouraging infections.

'Women have a great advantage that they may take up with little things without disgracing themselves; a man cannot, except with fiddling.' *Samuel Johnson*

Hair-raising

If your funds are limited, spend all you have on one really good cut rather than all the fancy (and overpriced) products on the market.

If you've got longish hair, why not have your hairdresser put it up, à la Audrey Hepburn? And wear some dangly earrings to add to that sophisticated look.

If your hair is thinning, go for a shorter, blunter cut to give the illusion of thickness.

Make your own egg shampoo by mixing two eggs and half an eggshell of olive oil. Massage into your scalp and rinse thoroughly.

Heal and prevent split ends by rubbing corn oil into your hair, making sure the ends are covered. Leave on for several minutes, then rinse your hair.

Reduce split ends by using a pure bristle brush.

Give your hair a really deep condition by massaging in lots of mayonnaise and then leaving it on for 10 minutes before rinsing off.

To give your hair a treat, warm a couple of tablespoons of olive or almond oil in a cup (more if your hair is very long). Rub into your hair and then wrap your head in cling film. Cover with a warm towel and leave for at least half an hour, but much longer if you can manage it – try not to answer the door! Shampoo and rinse.

For a refreshing hair tonic, take a few sprigs of rosemary and cut up finely. Put into 10 fl oz/300 ml water and bring to the boil. Simmer for 10 minutes and leave to go cold. To use, dip a piece of linen into the infusion and rub over your scalp.

If you run out of hair conditioner, fabric conditioner will do just as well.

If you suffer from dandruff, place one tea-spoon of parsley and an egg in a cup and beat together. Massage into your hair and leave for 5 minutes, then rinse out thoroughly.

Another good cure for dandruff is to put about 10 or 12 stinging-nettle heads into a bowl. Pour boiling water over them and leave to cool. Strain so that any bits are removed. The leftover liquid can be used as a final rinse after shampooing.

Don't buy expensive dandruff shampoos – just add some olive oil to your conditioner.

A natural way of darkening your hair is to get a handful of sage leaves, cover with a tea-spoon of borax and 10 fl oz/300 ml of boiling water. Let this mixture grow cold and then apply it carefully to your hair with a brush. Leave for twenty minutes and wash out.

If you have long, lank hair, try drying it with your head upside down to get more lift and body.

Make your own styling wax – use petro-leum jelly.

For an alternative setting lotion, use pale ale.

'Women's liberation will not be achieved until a woman can become paunchy and bald and still think she's attractive to the opposite sex.' *Earl Wilson*

Smelling Good

Always try a new perfume when you walk through the beauty department of a store. Try and experiment with a new one every time.

Make sure your perfume is working for you – always apply it to your pulse points (behind the ears, nape of the neck, inside the wrists, the temples, the crook of the elbow, behind the knees and on the ankles).

Perfume rises, so putting it on your lower body works well.

Spray your writing paper with your favourite perfume and keep it in a box. You will enjoy the fragrance when you go to write a letter and your friends will enjoy it, too.

The higher the concentration of perfume, the longer the scent lasts – extrait de parfum or perfume has the highest concentration, followed by parfum de toilette and eau de parfum, then eau de toilette, eau de cologne and, lowest of all, splash cologne.

Dress It Up

All dressed up and nowhere to go? So what?! Every now and again, get really dressed up in your best bib and tucker, pour yourself a glass of wine and enjoy feeling like a million dollars.

'Women dress alike all over the world; they dress to be annoying to other women.' *Elsa Schiaparelli*

Wear your clothes, don't let them wear you. Do you want people to remember you or the figure-hugging, leopard-print, low-cut blouse and leather miniskirt outfit?

Don't leave getting dressed up to the last minute. Always try on that little black dress, or favourite suit or whatever you had planned to wear for that special occasion, at least two days before. You may find your outfit needs a few alterations or even, worst-case scenario, a complete re-think. You don't want to be standing in front of the mirror, with twenty minutes to get ready, and find that you can't do the zip up on your party frock!

If you are a working mum, avoid florals – they just look too mumsy.

Never carry shopping bags to a meeting. Buy a smart leather 'shopper' that can carry papers as well as a pint of milk without giving the game away.

Take trouble over shoes and hosiery. Make sure they match and are in good condition.

Wear perfume, not eau de baby wipe.

Check your handbag and remove pea-shooters, stickers, dummies and anything else you might pull out when hunting for a pen.

Make sure your clothes and accessories are in proportion to your build. Large-framed, tall women should go for looser-fitting clothes, medium to bold prints, medium to large accessories and longer lengths, whereas small and petite women should choose neat-fitting clothes in fine to medium-weight fabrics, patterns only on the top half (if at all), and average to small accessories.

Black can look jarring on people with soft,

rounded features, so choose darker versions of warm tones, such as browns and khaki greens.

Overly baggy clothes can look shapeless – aim to flatter curves rather than disguise them completely.

Worried about your hips? Look out for shirts and jackets that sit just below the hips as they are very slimming. Avoid boxy jackets – they draw attention to wide hips.

For instantly longer legs, choose skirts and trousers with a small slit up the side which give the illusion of length and slenderness.

Skirts should always end at a flattering (slim) point of your leg.

Front pleats are a nightmare – flat-fronted trousers and skirts avoid extra bulk.

If you're petite, avoid wearing more than two colours or two garments at the same time as this will make you look cluttered and smaller than you are.

Columns of colour give the illusion of extra height; and wearing a darker colour on your bottom half is more slimming.

If you are of angular build, choose fabrics that drape softly over waist and hips. Stiff fabrics and block shapes can look harsh. It's also worth exploring colours such as rust or cinnamon – which suggest approachability – rather than black.

If you are a classic English pear shape and find skirts hard to buy, go for an A-line style, which falls around or just below the knee and which has some pleating or fluting towards the hem.

Wear a V neck for a slimmer-looking neck-line.

To make your bust look larger, dust a little bit of blusher on your cleavage.

To draw attention away from a large bust, wear a very simple, plain white shirt.

To draw attention away from your hips, wear a scarf around your neck.

Stop the hem of your silk skirt or sari from flying away – sew a 2-pence piece into the hem.

Make zips work more efficiently by running a lead pencil along the metal teeth.

'Money isn't everything but it sure keeps you in touch with your children.' *J. Paul Getty*

When it comes to choosing new clothes, buy for today's weight, not your goal weight. If it doesn't flatter now, you won't get the use out of it.

Don't buy a skirt or trousers that you

wouldn't be prepared to wear without a jacket.

If you wear a trouser suit, you'll have to be better groomed to look as professional as a woman in a skirt suit.

What you wear underneath affects the whole look. Ensure that you are wearing underwear that fits.

A fashionable handbag and pair of shoes will update a classic look with minimum investment.

Coats and jackets get seen first, so make sure yours is the very best you can afford. Buy a classic expensive one in a sale where you will get the best value.

When looking for a really glamorous evening dress, it's a good idea to be fitted for a fabulous bra which will give you the shape you love, then buy the dress to show off your shape. (Needless to say, always try on the dress wearing your super bra.)

A very French tip – buy one or two things of really good quality and keep the rest very simple. A good pair of shoes and a decent haircut (regularly maintained) are true style secrets.

Once you have discovered a clothing style that suits you, stick to it. You can update your look with the latest shoes and bags each season.

When buying an expensive new handbag, always fill it to see how it looks (some bags look ugly when packed) and try it on in front of a mirror to check that its proportions suit yours.

To prevent fluff from your angora jumper getting all over the inside of a jacket, put the jumper in the freezer before wearing it. Alternatively, give your mohair and angora woollies the occasional squirt of hairspray to stop them from moulting.

Get rid of static electricity by running a wire coat hanger over the offending garment.

To get a jacket to hang straight, put pennies (or spare foreign coins) into the bottom of the hem.

Remove the shine from velvet, wool or viscose by spraying the affected area with water and then leaving to dry. Give the material a good brush when it's completely dry.

Get rid of fluff and cat hairs by wrapping sticky tape around your hand and rubbing up and down the item of clothing.

Milk-stained clothes – a hazard of being a mother – should be rinsed in cool water. Then washed in cold water using liquid detergent.

Planning to make yourself a stunning new outfit? When choosing a pattern, it's more important to get the right measurement for the bust than for the hips. The hip measurements are normally much easier to adjust.

When drawing patterns, especially tricky curves, be bold and draw quickly. You'll achieve a much smoother line than if you go at it more cautiously.

To achieve the best possible fit start making adjustments at the neckline and shoulders as these will affect the whole hang and style of a garment.

When trying on a garment that you're making, make it easier by putting it on inside out. Adjust it accordingly, tack it up and then try it on again the right way round.

A waistline will be much more flattering if it dips slightly at the back.

To make a small bust look fuller, use long darts round the chest area.

If you're looking for a practical fabric, try squashing it in your hand to see how easily it will crease.

Fabric tape-measures often stretch. This can leave you with inaccurate measurements. For accuracy, buy a fibreglass or coated one.

Don't make your thread too long. The longer the thread, the more it gets weakened as it's drawn through the fabric. Shorter threads are less work – your arm doesn't have to move as much!

Put synthetic thread in the fridge for a couple of hours before you use it. This will stop it clinging to the fabric.

Always cut thread at an angle.

If you're finding it hard to push the needle through a fabric, rub some soap over the cloth on the wrong side.

Always keep a spool of clear thread for emergency repairs when you can't match any of your threads with a fabric.

Use an old tailor's trick and rub your needle along the side of your nose. It picks up just enough grease to 'oil' its passage through the fabric.

Keep your sewing machine needle sharp – stitch it through some fine sandpaper for a few inches.

'If women dressed for men, the clothes store wouldn't sell much – just the odd sun visor' *Groucho Marx*

Keep creases in your trousers for longer. Put soap on the inside of the crease when pressing your trouser leg. Alternatively, to put a good, long-lasting crease in trousers, apply a thin line of paper glue along the inside of the crease and then iron it.

Iron items that need a cool iron first. Gradually work through the ironing, finishing with items that need a hotter setting.

If your pile of ironing has become bone dry, pop it back into the tumble dryer with a wet towel for a minute. This will get items slightly damp again and they will be easier to iron. If you don't have a tumble dryer, wrap them in a wet towel instead.

To remove fabric shine, dampen a cloth and wring out the excess water. Put this cloth on top of the shiny fabric and steam press. Do this several times, pressing the area until it is almost dry.

Put a drop of essential oil into your steam iron water to make clothes smell nice.

Ironing on the reverse side of clothes keeps the colour longer.

Protect delicate buttons when ironing – place a metal spoon over them.

If buttons have a habit of popping off, dab a bit of clear nail varnish over the button thread to strengthen the fibres.

Hang a wet, clean white shirt outside on a cold morning and it will come up bright white.

If your iron sticks to your clothes, wrap a bar of soap in a hanky and rub it over the hot face of the iron – it will be as smooth as when it was new.

For a rusty iron, tie a piece of beeswax

inside a rag and rub the iron when hot. Then rub with another rag sprinkled with salt.

To shift limescale from a steam iron, simply fill the water tank with cider vinegar, turn the iron to 'steam' and run it over a soft cloth for several minutes. You will need to rinse out the inside of your iron thoroughly afterwards.

Starch can get stuck to the sole plate of an iron – to remove it, run the iron over a piece of kitchen foil.

When ironing delicate fabrics place tissue paper over the top.

Avoid ironing silk and velvet altogether – both will lose their creases if hung in a steamy bathroom.

Wash silk garments after every wear, otherwise perspiration stains may be impossible to remove and will actually weaken the fabric.

When washing silk, a couple of lumps of sugar added to the final rinse will give the silk more body and make life sweeter.

Keep jackets and long-sleeved dresses looking like new by stuffing the sleeves with crumpled-up tissue paper.

Firm Foundations

'I was the first woman to burn my bra ... it took the fire department four days to put it out.' *Dolly Parton*

At least 75 per cent of women wear the wrong size of bra, so the chances are you're one of them.

If a bra is properly fitted, you shouldn't be aware that you're wearing it. If you can't wait to get it off, you're in the wrong size.

You only want to have two breasts. If it looks as if you have four, your cup size is too small.

Wrinkling all over the cup, especially at the top and sides, means the cup size is too big. The breasts should be enclosed in the cups with a smooth silhouette.

The front and back of a bra should be at the same level and shouldn't budge. If the bra rides up at the back, it can't be support- ing you properly and it is probably too big. Choose one with a smaller back and a bigger cup size.

Underwired bras give better separation, support and lift, and give a better line under clothes. Soft-cup bras are fine for maternity, breast-feeding, sports and mastectomy bras.

If underwired bras dig in at the side of

the breast or stick out, the cup size is too small. Many women complain of this, but once they've been properly fitted, they're converted.

If you have marks on your shoulders from your bra straps, the bra is not giving your breasts enough support.

Stop bras from rubbing by soaking them regularly in hair conditioner.

To prevent bra straps from showing fix Velcro strips to your bra and on the inside of the dress strap.

Pure cotton is not the best fabric for a bra as it stretches. You should aim for a maximum of 30 to 40 per cent cotton, and always have a bit of elastane.

A bra will last six months to a year, depending on how you treat it. If little bits of elastic start appearing at the back, it's high time to chuck it.

Handwash bras, rinse well, don't wring underwires and always drip dry.

Bras hate heat, so don't wash them in a machine, never put them in a tumble dryer and never hang them over radiators.

Bra size does not necessarily carry across from make to make, so try on different sizes. If you are, say, a 36C, go down a back size and up a cup size to 34D, then up a back size and down a cup size to 38B to find the best fit in other makes.

The adjuster straps over the shoulders need tightening with wear. It's very hard to get these even yourself, so ask a trusted friend.

For bigger boobs, wear fitted or stream-lined shapes, as these are much more flattering than baggy clothes. Look for fitted tops with seams or darts under the bust as these will define your waist.

Round, scooped or V necklines tend to be more flattering for bigger boobs than high necklines.

Wear plain colours to minimise a big bust – avoid busy patterns, large prints and patch pockets.

Keep tops light and bottoms dark to emphasise boobs, and darker tops and lighter bottoms to draw the attention away.

Wear jewellery away from your bust – it's more flattering around your neck than on your boobs.

Wear a good sports bra. There are no muscles in the breasts and once you stretch the ligaments and they become damaged there is nothing you can do short of surgery.

Make sure you find a good basque or strapless bra before you commit yourself to a strapless dress, especially if you have a big bust.

Lacy bras are sexy, but aren't so good under a very fitted evening or wedding dress.

Get your breasts re-measured every 6 to 8 months, and monthly when you're pregnant. Get fitted for a nursing bra as close to your due date as possible.

If your breasts enlarge before your period, get measured then, too, and have a couple of larger bras so you're comfy all month. Premenstrual tension and a tight bra – definitely to be avoided!

Every woman needs between 4 and 8 bras. They must be washed every day, like knickers, and worn in rotation to ensure a long and supportive life.

Hats Off

Hats are not just for Ascot. They don't have to be huge creations with feathers and bows. You can wear a hat when you go shopping or picking the children up from school. Just make sure it reflects your personality . . . and wear it with attitude!

'Never despise what it says in women's magazines . . . it may not be subtle but neither are men.' *Zsa Zsa Gabor*

Always try a hat on standing up and walking about so that you can assess the whole outline and not just the head and shoulders.

Big shoulders can be made to look smaller by wearing smaller, neater hats.

The best hat for heart-shaped faces is one with a medium brim worn at an angle.

For those with square faces, choose a wide-brimmed hat.

For those with long faces, hats that have curved brims with some decoration look best.

Those with round faces should choose hats that are deep-crowned and worn low on the head. If you can't find this sort of hat, tilt any other sort of hat at an angle.

To measure the size of your head correctly, take your tape-measure around from the centre of the forehead, behind the ear, over the bump at the back of the head, behind the other ear and back to the front.

If the final hat is going to be made from a thick fabric such as velvet, add 1 in/2.5 cm to the measurements.

To avoid a lopsided look, the front brim of a hat should always be wider than the back.

If you have a long neck, a wide-brimmed hat will suit you best.

Straw hat gone floppy? Brush over the

inside with a thin layer of cellulose varnish, which will dry quickly, but stay flexible enough for you to manipulate the brim.

If you want a straw hat to remain completely rigid, brush it with a thin layer of clear varnish or picture varnish and leave it to dry. This also gives a glossy look.

For a quick new look for a straw hat, spray with oil- or acrylic-based paint.

To bring up the colour on a white or cream felt hat, sprinkle with talcum powder.

Sprinkle a white or cream felt hat with bran. Leave it overnight, then brush it off in the morning. This works like an exfoliator.

To revive flowers on a hat, shake them over a steaming kettle and they'll blossom back into life.

Don't mess up expensive ribbon by practising how to tie it. Play around with some muslin instead until you are sure where and how you want the bow.

Beautiful Baubles

'No pressure. No diamonds.' *Mary Case*

Pearls of wisdom

Be Grace Kelly (or Coco Chanel) for the day – wear pearls. If you can't afford the real thing, there are all kinds of fake pearls to be had for a pittance.

To test whether pearls are real or not, simply place them between your teeth. Real pearls have a gritty surface; fake pearls are smooth.

Real pearls should be worn regularly so that they can absorb the moisture from your body that will keep them looking lustrous. They should be the first thing to go on in the morning and the last thing to come off at night.

Don't wear your pearls in the shower – the silk thread will become damaged and rot.

If your string of pearls breaks, pick up all the pearls and put them on a round tea tray. You can then use the curve to sort the pearls out so that they are in the right order for restringing.

Wash real pearls in very salty water. Leave them to dry and then polish with a piece of velvet.

Shine pearls with a dab of olive oil and wipe dry with a chamois.

Clean artificial pearls with a chamois leather. Just rub it carefully over the beads.

Clean and sparkly

For a good, general jewellery cleaner, try

a weak solution of washing-up liquid in warm water with a drop of household ammonia.

Don't be conned into buying expensive gold cleaners: most are just variations on common household bleach.

Useful cleaning tools are old toothbrushes and mascara wands.

Some stones shouldn't be put in cleaning solution: jade, coral and lapis lazuli only need a gentle polish. Opals and turquoise are fragile so polish carefully with a cloth.

Costume jewellery can still be expensive. Look after yours by cleaning it with a little baking powder, then brushing off any residue with a soft toothbrush.

Next time you clean your watch, remove the scratches on the face, too. Just spend 5 or 10 minutes gently rubbing the glass with metal polish, then wipe it off with a soft duster.

Bring a shine to tortoiseshell by rubbing it with almond oil.

To remove marks from tortoiseshell, rub talcum powder over the mark with a cotton rag.

Clean amber in some warm milk, dry, and polish with a soft silk cloth.

Jet can be cleaned with soft breadcrumbs.

You can wash jade from time to time in soapy warm water. Jade should be handled as much as possible.

Emeralds are naturally fragile – always get them cleaned professionally.

Never put your emeralds in hot water: the gems will absorb the liquid and crack.

If your emeralds dry out, pour a little almond oil on the stones, wrap them in a towel and leave them on the radiator overnight.

Opals are very porous, so avoid washing them altogether. Instead buff them up with a soft chamois leather.

To clean coral jewellery, lightly sponge with a weak detergent solution.

If your diamonds have lost their sparkle, drop them into a glass of water, add one denture-cleaning tablet and leave them to soak for a couple of minutes.

Gold chains need careful handling. Soapy water is the best thing to clean them with but try rubbing the gold gently in a chamois leather afterwards to make them really sparkle.

To make gold sparkle, soak your piece of jewellery for several minutes in gin. Treat yourself to a G&T while you wait!

To prevent your gold rings from getting misshapen, dented or scratched, cover your car steering wheel with some soft foam or fabric. Apparently, gripping the wheel too tight is the most common cause of damage.

The best way to bring up a 9-carat shine is with a soft-bristled toothbrush.

The best thing to buff up gold jewellery is a spectacle-cleaning cloth.

To maintain a gleam, remove all gold before bathing. The soapy water simply builds up a film and your precious jewellery will soon look dull.

To store your gold and silver without damage, line your jewellery box with an empty egg tray, so you can keep each piece of jewellery in a separate compartment.

To stop jewellery becoming tarnished, place a piece of chalk in your trinket box.

Clean silver jewellery by coating with a little toothpaste (not gel or stripy), then leave for an hour or so and rub off with a dry cloth.

To stop silver jewellery from tarnishing, wrap in black tissue.

Cameos should never be immersed in water. Use a brush dipped in warm soapy water and brush the surface gently. Rinse in the same way with clean water. Blot off excess water and rub with a chamois leather.

Store earrings by poking them through a piece of fabric.

Lost the butterfly from the back of your earring? Use a piece of pencil rubber as a temporary measure.

If you are getting a rash from a piece of jewellery but can't bear to get rid of it, try cleaning it first, then apply a coat of clear nail varnish to all the parts that touch your skin.

To stop stones falling out of your costume jewellery, paint them with clear nail varnish.

Shoes – You Can Never Have Too Many

'Despite my thirty years of research into the feminine soul, I have not been able to answer . . . the great question that has never been answered: what does a woman want?'
Sigmund Freud

Well, a fair proportion of women want shoes . . . and more shoes. So many shoes, so little time. How many pairs of shoes do you have in your wardrobe? Bet it's more than one. If you are the archetypal woman, you should have a few pairs to choose from. Be kind to your shoes. Don't make them work too hard. Give them a rest, don't wear a pair of shoes day in, day out.

If your shoes are a bit tight stuff them
with potato skins and leave overnight.

New shoes often rub at the heel. Make
sure yours are comfy from day one. Place the
heel of the shoe over the arm of a wooden
chair, cover with some cardboard and then
bash with a hammer . . . it's a bit like ten-
derising meat!

The best way to soften leather is to wrap
it in a soft cloth and then soak it in water
overnight.

If you've got big feet, stick to dark or
neutral colours. White or bright colours will
only draw attention to them.

If you've got narrow feet, shoe flaps sometimes slip over each other. To prevent this
happening, simply place a bit of felt under
the flaps before you lace the shoes up.

**Save your energy and polish your shoes
in the evening** and then buff them up the
next morning. This gives a better finish
anyway.

To make leather shoes last longer try
using some saddle soap in place of ordinary
cleaning products.

If you've run out of shoe polish, you can
use floor wax, furniture polish or window-
cleaning spray.

For an alternative brown shoe polish, rub

the inside of a banana skin along the leather. Leave to dry and don't buff them up.

Polish black shoes with the inside of the rind of a fresh orange.

Canvas shoes often look grubby very quickly. Carpet shampoo, applied with a small brush, will make them look as good as new.

Prevent your shoes from scuffing by painting a layer of clear nail varnish on the heel and toe of your shoes.

Keep your suede shoes looking pristine by removing any marks with an eraser.

Freshen up old suede shoes by giving them a good steam over the kettle.

Nubuck shoes quickly lose their downy roughness. To make them furry again, rub gently with some fine sandpaper.

Get rid of salt marks during the winter by mixing one tablespoon of vinegar in one cup of water and then wiping over the marks.

Never wear new leather shoes in the rain. They need a bit of wear, tear and cleaning to build up water resistance.

For an effective waterproof coating give your shoes a final polish with a coat of floor wax.

If your shoes get soaked, take them off as soon as you get home and stuff them with newspaper. Leave them to dry naturally; don't try to speed the process up by putting them in front of a fire or in bright sunshine. When they are dry, use some saddle soap to condition them and then polish.

To dry wellies, use a hair dryer.

Dyed shoes often mark your feet when they get wet. Prevent this from happening by spraying the inside of the shoe with some Scotchguard.

If you've got marks on your white stilettos, try getting rid of them with nail varnish remover. If you can't get them off this way, dab some correcting fluid over the marks. Alternatively, remove black marks from white leather shoes by gently rubbing with a damp Brillo pad.

Stiletto heels always get scuffed and marked. Try spraying them with some matching car paint as a durable solution.

Scuff marks can be covered by gently building up layers of felt-tip pen until you reach the perfect colour match.

Make patent leather sparkle with furniture polish. Alternatively, bring the shine back to patent leather – try rubbing a little vegetable or baby oil over the shoe and then buff with some kitchen paper towel.

Patent-leather shoes also come up a treat if rubbed over with petroleum jelly.

Deodorise trainers by filling the feet of pop socks with unused cat litter, tie the ends, place inside and leave overnight.

Even the grubbiest of trainers look fit for Centre Court if you give them a good clean with a baby wipe.

To clean the white rubber areas (the 'bumpers') on training shoes, use toothpaste.

If your leather laces are a bit wide for the holes, dampen them first and then pull them through a small hole punched in some cardboard before trying to lace them up in the actual shoe.

To stop shoe laces coming undone wet them before you tie them. The knot will remain in place. Or you could wax the laces with polish before doing them up.

The plastic tips often come off laces and once frayed they're very difficult to thread through shoe holes. Pull the plastic tips off and just burn the ends to seal them for a permanent solution.

If the bottoms of your shoes feel sticky, sprinkle a little talcum powder over the sole.

If your soles are slippery, rub a piece of sandpaper across them. Or stick a piece of sandpaper to each one.

Place orange peel in a pair of smelly summer shoes overnight and they'll be much fresher the following day. Or you could try placing a fabric-softener sheet in them.

When you get your sandals out of the wardrobe after a long winter, they often feel really stiff and uncomfortable. Pop them in the oven for 3 or 4 minutes at 210°F/100°C and they will soon soften up.

If your boots are really tight, put your foot into a small plastic bag and it will slip into the boot more easily. Once you've got the boot on, you can tear off the bag.

Stop your shoes losing their shape at the toes – keep your toenails short.

Successful Shopping

'When you have only two pennies left in the world, buy a loaf of bread with one, and a lily with the other.' *Chinese proverb*

When the going gets tough, the tough go shopping. There's shopping for groceries, children's clothes and cat food. And there's shopping for you. Which one do you think we're going to recommend here?

Experimenting with a new look? Don't do it by buying expensive items. Get the look right first before you break the bank.

Try not to go shopping with people who

are younger, thinner or richer than you are. You will only get depressed and over-spend to make yourself feel better. (Daughters are the exception . . . they should remind you of what fabulous genes you have passed on!)

Leave the children at home.

In fact it's probably best if you don't take anyone with you. You'll get a lot more done on your own and it's important to make it a special time for yourself.

Shopping and alcohol are a bad combination; do not mix the two.

Avoid nasty changing rooms with bad lighting. Nobody can feel good in that kind of atmosphere.

Try to avoid shopping for clothes when it's your time of the month. You'll be carrying a few extra pounds anyway, and probably not feeling at your most gorgeous. So don't depress yourself.

For an instant treat, go and get 'made-up' at a department store.

When buying new shoes, shop for them at the end of the day when your feet are at their largest. If you buy shoes in the morning, they can become uncomfortable later on in the day.

Always try on both shoes because most

people have one foot slightly smaller than the other.

'The place of the father in the modern suburban family is a very small one, particularly if he plays golf.' *Bertrand Russell*

Out and About

'With this so-called nouvelle cuisine there is nothing on your plate and plenty on your bill.' *Paul Bocuse*

You may get taken out for a meal on Mother's Day, you may even be taken away for the weekend. Here are a few tips for when you are on the road and travelling . . .

Don't be intimidated by posh hotels. You may not have the budget to book a room, but there's nothing to stop you from having a drink in the bar or a coffee in the lounge as you while away an hour or two, watching the world go by. Also, always spend a bit of time in the ladies loo. There are usually gorgeous soaps, hand lotions, even perfumes, to play with.

If you are going out somewhere busy with the family, like a crowded park or funfair, tie a brightly coloured balloon to the pushchair. That way, if the family gets split up, you'll be able to find one another more easily.

If you turn up at a restaurant having booked a table to be told they haven't actually got one for you, the restaurant is in breach of contract and you're entitled to compensation.

And there is such a thing as a free lunch – a restaurant is actually obliged to ask you if you enjoyed your meal. If they fail to do this and you didn't really enjoy the food, you are not liable to pay the bill.

Travelling by road? Prevent car sickness – chew some crystallised ginger.

Remove creases from silk with a hair dryer after a long journey. If you're on the road, you can always use a hot-air hand dryer in a service station.

'A suburban mother's role is to deliver children – obstetrically once and by car forever.' *Peter De Vries*

If you are going off on a holiday break, leave half a lemon in each of your rooms at home to keep them smelling sweet.

If you are travelling abroad, check with your doctor about any inoculations you might need.

Never put your home address on luggage labels. When you arrive at the airport, it only advertises the fact that you are away on holiday for a while and that your house is unoccupied. Put your address inside your suitcase.

Mark your luggage with a ribbon or cord

(or funny sticker if you are travelling with children) so that you can spot it easily as it comes around on the carousel.

Spread your children's possessions around the family's luggage – just in case one case goes missing, you should have some of the things that they need.

Combat jet lag on long plane journeys with a ballpoint pen. Take the blunt end of the pen and press it into the ball of your big toe several times; this massages the pressure point and relieves tiredness and nausea.

Avoid puffy eyes when flying. Place a couple of slices of cucumber over your closed eyes.

Take a clothes hanger with you, because in many hotels you can't take the hangers out of the wardrobes. You'll find it useful to be able to hang clothes in the bathroom.

If you get sunburnt and you've run out of cream, dab on some neat vinegar to ease the pain.

The Perfect Mother's Day Meal

If you are lucky, you will get taken out for a meal (see pp. 57–9 for hints and tips on that). You might have the meal cooked for you. Or perhaps you will find yourself in the kitchen, cooking a Mother's Day meal for the whole family! Wasn't this supposed to be your day? Never mind, here are some handy hints and tips, designed to take the stress out of the occasion, to make any Mother's Day celebration lunch (or any special meal for that matter) go with a swing.

'He's a perfectionist. If he was married to Raquel Welch he'd expect her to cook.' *Don Meredith*

Don't feel you have to do all the cooking for a celebration meal. If your family ask if they can bring anything, suggest they bring a pudding – whatever the family favourites are.

People usually try too hard when entertaining. Stick to dishes you have made before rather than launching into an ambitious recipe plucked out of a book. And don't try to put together a really exotic menu – if the main course is rich, try some sliced melon for starters. Likewise, if fancy puds are your thing, serve a simple main course of grilled fish or steak and salad.

Use music to change the mood when entertaining. Something pacy will get you moving in the kitchen, but then slow things down with something relaxing so you can enjoy your meal with everyone else.

If you want your guests to be comfortable, remember to set your heating thermostat a few degrees lower than usual. All those bodies will create their own heat.

Setting the Scene

'I can't cook; I use a smoke alarm as a timer.' *Carol Siskind*

If you are worried about staining your wooden table, put some cling film across the table top before putting on the tablecloth. If you are concerned about hot dishes marking the wood, put a blanket underneath the tablecloth.

A simple way to create a circular tablecloth is to fold your material in half. Take a piece of string (no longer than the width of the folded material), attach a pencil to one end and a drawing pin to the other. Stick the drawing pin on the edge of the fold, draw a semicircle over the fabric and cut out.

Tablecloths can look elegant if trimmed with braid or tassels. However, it can be expensive to trim all the way round a piece of fabric. Instead, decorate the edges of a much smaller top cloth.

Candles

To keep night-light candles burning for ages put a pinch of salt in each one.

Candles add atmosphere to a meal. Make sure yours are below eye-level though so that your guests can actually see each other.

Always set your dining room table with candles. Apart from looking pretty, they give off a special smell.

To make candles burn brightly, soak the wicks in vinegar.

If you get candle wax on your tablecloth, heat a spoon over the candle, then place a piece of wet newspaper over the wax and rub the hot spoon over the newspaper to melt the wax. It will come off the tablecloth and stick to the paper.

To stop candles dripping, sharpen the ends like a pencil. This stops the wax from collecting in a pool and then suddenly spilling over.

Candles burn more evenly and won't drip if you pop them in a freezer before use.

Spray candles with your favourite perfume. As they burn down, they release the smell into the room. Ideal for candlelit dinners!

Yellow will make the room feel sunny, pink will create a dramatic, warm effect and orange will give it a warm and welcoming feel.

Warm and glistening

Don't panic if you've forgotten to heat the plates. Just splash with hot water and pop them in the microwave for a few seconds (check that your china is microwaveable first). Alternatively, warm plates for the meal in the drying cycle of your dishwasher.

To make your plates gleam like new, rinse in a weak solution of water and vinegar.

Good-quality china will really sparkle if soaked in denture-cleaning tablets.

Thirteen guests for dinner can be unlucky, so put a teddy bear on a fourteenth chair!

Polish up cutlery using a cork soaked in water and scouring powder. Rinse and buff with a soft cloth.

Fabulous Food

'I am a light eater ... as soon as it is light I start to eat.' *Art Donovan*

If you always get in a mess with cling film, try storing it in the fridge. It's easier to use when cold.

Line kitchen scales with cling film before weighing out ingredients, so you don't need to wash them afterwards. The correct amount also goes into the mixture rather than staying in the scales – great for sticky butter!

If your hands are stained, rub with a piece of raw potato. This works on kitchen work-tops, too.

If nuts are difficult to crack, try freezing

them first. Alternatively, put them in cold water and bring them to the boil for a few minutes.

Soups and sauces

To avoid lumpy white sauce, heat the milk first.

To thicken gravy, add instant mashed potato powder.

When making stocks or gravy, put a chip basket inside the pan to hold bones, bay leaves and other chunky ingredients. This will make it easier to lift them all out when you have finished.

To stop oil or butter from spitting in a frying pan, sprinkle in a pinch of salt when adding the oil/butter.

When making soup put a crustless piece of bread in the blender with the other ingredients to give the soup a lovely texture.

If you want to make the soup go further, add wine, cream or stock. This will enhance the flavour as well.

To thicken homemade soup, just add some instant mashed potato before serving. Alternatively, to thicken stews and soups, don't use flour – porridge oats are very effective and much tastier, too.

To get rid of congealed fat in a soup or stew, drop in an ice cube. It should attract the excess grease to it, gathering it in one place for you to remove.

Jazz up plain tinned soup by stirring in some sherry or port.

Pep up boring bean or vegetable soup with a large spoonful of balsamic vinegar.

A dash of lemon juice added to cream of mushroom soup just before serving will cut through the richness of the soup and bring out the full flavour.

Draw a slice of bread across soups or stews to soak up excess grease.

When serving soup to children, stir an ice cube into their portions to cool it down quickly.

If your hollandaise sauce curdles, gently stir in an ice cube.

A spoonful of cream added to a sauce made with milk will give the impression that it's all made with cream.

To make a tasty dip, mix half a packet of mushroom or onion soup with a small carton of cream and chill for a few hours.

Bread

To keep bread rolls warm when served in

a bread basket, line the basket with foil and then cover with a napkin.

Freshen bread rolls for breakfast by covering them with a damp towel and placing them in a hot oven for a short while.

To make neat butter curls, freeze the butter for a few minutes first.

If you need softened butter but have forgotten to take it out of the fridge, try grating it on to a warm dish.

The secret of fantastic bread is always to keep a little bit of dough back from the previous day's batch to add to the new mixture.

To prevent bread from drying out when baking, cover it with a cake tin while it's in the oven.

Don't throw day-old bread away, just brush it with olive oil and toast it in the oven.

It's easier to cut pizza with scissors than with a knife.

To keep bread moist while baking, add a little honey to the dough.

To keep home-baked bread fresh for longer, add a couple of teaspoons of vegetable oil to the dough.

When kneading dough, stop every 2 or 3 minutes to let the dough 'rest'. After resting for a couple of minutes, the dough will be easier to knead. The longer you knead dough, the longer you should leave the dough to develop.

If you can't remember whether you've added yeast to your dough, here's a simple test. Take out a small piece of the dough – about gobstopper size – and put it in a cup of hot water. If you didn't put in any yeast, it will immediately sink to the bottom. Dough with yeast in it will rise to the top.

Flour compacts during storage. Fluff it up before measuring out an amount for a recipe or you'll get too much flour.

To test whether a loaf of homemade bread is baked properly tap it on top. A hollow sound means that it is baked.

Place a wet towel over your dough when making bread to make it rise more quickly.

If, when heating or baking bread at home, the bread burns and/or has burnt spots on it, cut the spots off and patch up the scars with beaten egg brushed on to the exposed areas. Then keep heating the bread.

Dried-out, stale bread can be revived if you wrap it in kitchen foil and leave on a low heat in the oven for about 10 minutes. Alternatively, plunge the loaf or rolls into cold water for a moment and then bake on a low heat for ten minutes.

Never run out of breadcrumbs for stuffings and toppings – keep all your bread ends, pop into a food processor to make crumbs and then freeze in bags.

Pastries

For savoury pies, add a little pesto to flavour the pastry – delicious!

To prevent soggy quiche bases, brush the pastry with lemon juice and bake blind for 3 minutes before putting the filling in and cooking fully.

When cooking vol-au-vents, don't put them in straight lines on your baking tray. Instead, place them randomly but close together and they will lift each other up while cooking.

To stop cakes and pastries sticking to shaped cutters, brush the insides of the cutters with a little oil.

To store vol-au-vents, sprinkle a thin layer of salt on the bottom of a cake tin, cover with a tea towel and place your vol-au-vents on the cloth. They will stay fresh for ages.

Before putting puff pastry on a baking tray, run ice-cold water over the tray. When it is in the oven, the steam rising from the tray will really help the pastry to puff.

Not for Vegetarians

'Men like to barbecue ... men like to cook only if danger is involved.' *Rita Rudner*

If you're tight on oven space, all meats can be half cooked the day before, stored in the fridge and then finished off when needed.

As an alternative to honey-roast ham, try emptying a can of Coca-Cola into the baking tray for a really sweet-tasting meat.

To roast a turkey evenly, begin roasting it upside down and only turn it right side up after about 45 minutes.

To stop a turkey sticking to tin foil during cooking, place a piece of celery along the breastbone.

When grilling lots of sausages, thread them on to skewers so that it's easier to keep turning them.

Your bacon will be really crispy if you trim the rind with pinking shears before cooking it.

Does the meat seem a bit tough? Squirt a little lemon juice on to it before carving.

For a low-fat gravy, try separating the meat juices and fat by pouring them into a jug and adding ice cubes. The ice will cool down the gravy quickly, allowing you to spoon off the fat straight away.

Make your own marinade for pork: use a tablespoon of honey mixed with grated ginger – sweet and spicy.

To skim the grease off stock during cooking, drop in a cold piece of lettuce for 10 seconds. The grease in the hot stock will stick to the lettuce leaf. Alternatively, if there's too much fat on the top of your casserole or sauce, gently float a piece of kitchen paper across the top and it will soak up the excess.

To tenderise meat cover it with slices of kiwi fruit for about 15 minutes.

To tenderise the meat in stews, add 3 or 4 wine corks to the pot. The corks release chemicals that both tenderise the meat and reduce cooking time. Just remember to remove them before serving!

To get the skin off chicken more easily, dip your hands in flour before trying to remove the skin. This will make the whole process much less slippery.

Keep poultry moist while roasting by placing a bowl of water in the bottom of the oven. Make sure you use a heatproof bowl or roasting tin.

Freeze meat in the coldest part of the freezer.

Roasting a chicken? Put some vegetables in a heatproof bowl and cook in the oven at the same time to save an additional ring on the cooker.

Marinating meat in distilled vinegar overnight tenderises it.

If you've overdone the chilli in your curry, squeeze half a lemon over it. Then place the half-lemon into the curry, stir for a few minutes and then remove. The strong chilli taste will have disappeared.

To rescue a casserole that has been over-salted, just add fizzy water. Or place a potato in the casserole for 10 minutes and then remove.

Something Fishy

'Govern a family as you would cook a small fish – very gently.' *Chinese proverb*

To ensure that you get the best range and quality of fish, choose a fishmonger that supplies local restaurants. The most important thing when buying fish is to ensure that it's really fresh.

Fresh fish should have a firm texture. Push your fingers into the flesh; if your indentation stays there, the fish is not really fresh.

To tell if a fish is fresh, check the brightness of the scales and the pinkness of the gills. The eyes must be clear, bright and not sunken. The tail of a truly fresh fish will be stiff.

Fresh sea fish should be bright and not noticeably dry.

Fresh trout should be slightly slimy to the touch.

Smoked fish should have a fresh smoky aroma and a glossy appearance.

Frozen fish should be frozen hard with no signs of partial thawing and the packaging should be undamaged.

For a really special treat, try caviar. The correct way to eat caviar is not with a silver spoon but from the back of your hand. It's even better if you use somebody else's hand!

To tell the difference between Oscietra and Beluga caviar put a few caviar eggs on a piece of paper and then crush them. If the oil is yellow, it's Oscietra, but if it's grey the caviar is Beluga.

Caviar can also be served on toast but the toast must be cold. Hot toast will make the eggs separate.

Don't buy plaice that has roe in it because it will be absolutely tasteless.

To tell if a salmon is wild or farmed, hold the tail between your thumb and forefinger. Farmed fish have far fewer scales and are more slippery. If it slips through your fingers, the fish is farmed.

Store fresh fish and smoked fish separately so that the flavours don't get mixed up.

Before freezing your fish, rinse it in water to create a protective glaze around the fish when it's frozen.

Before filleting and skinning fish, dip your fingers in salt. You'll get a much better grip.

Cut the fish from the bottom to the neck and then chop off the head. The innards will pull out easily.

Remove fiddly bones from salmon fillets with tweezers.

To remove the bones from raw fish, use a vegetable peeler. Run the peeler along the flesh, catching bones in the centre slit. Twist the peeler and pull the bones out.

Crab and lobster should feel heavier than you would expect. This means that they will be meaty and juicy.

Don't crush crab and lobster claws – use the handle of a teaspoon to get the meat out instead.

Pieces of bacon laid over skinned white fish fillets will keep them moist while cooking.

Cook fish in foil parcels to give delicious, moist morsels of fish.

You don't need an expensive steamer for fish, just put a colander over a pan of boiling water and cover the colander with a large lid.

Skinning fish is fiddly. Flash-grill the fish first under a very hot grill and the crispy, scorched skin will lift off effortlessly.

If you need only a couple of drops of lemon juice for fish, simply pierce the lemon with a cocktail stick and it will then stay fresh for use later.

To cook delicious juicy fish, wrap it in cling film and place in boiling water so that none of the natural flavour escapes.

To prevent fish skin from sticking to the frying pan rub the skin with salt, leave for 15 minutes, rinse and rub dry. Then cook.

To slice tuna thinly, pop it in the freezer for an hour beforehand.

To stop fish going soggy during cooking, sprinkle it with salt and leave for half an hour before cooking.

To clear fish guts and scales from your chopping board, use a window squeegee.

Mustard removes fishy smells from wooden boards.

Clean wooden chopping boards with half a lemon dipped in salt. This also prevents the surface from staining.

Ideally, clean fish on newspaper. This keeps your board clean and means you can wrap the waste up and put it straight into the bin.

To remove a fishy smell, rinse your hands in lemon juice.

Prevent that lingering fish smell on plates and in pots and pans by putting a tablespoon of vinegar in the washing-up water.

To clean a pan after cooking and to remove the fishy smell, leave some cold tea in the pan for 10 minutes before you wash it.

Viva Veg

'I eat merely to keep my mind off food.'
N. F. Simpson

If you overcook your vegetables, put them in icy-cold water for a few minutes and then microwave them very briefly before serving.

To prevent potatoes sprouting before you have a chance to use them, put an apple in the same bag as the spuds.

Prepare your potatoes the night before. To stop them becoming discoloured, leave them in a pan of water along with a small lump of rinsed coal. They will stay looking fresh until the next day.

The secret of crispy roast potatoes: once

they have been parboiled for about 5 minutes, drain well and put the lid back on the pan. Shake vigorously to fluff up the edges. Pour the potatoes on to very hot fat, and once they are cooked (for about one hour at 220°C, 425°F, gas 7), serve straight away.

If your roast potatoes take an age to brown, sprinkle a little flour over them as they cook.

You can have healthy roast potatoes! Parboil, then place on a baking tray lined with parchment paper. Roast in the top half of the oven.

For spuds that are high on flavour but low on calories, try drizzling some balsamic vinegar over cooked potatoes.

To stop potatoes falling apart while you boil them, turn the heat right down and boil them for longer, rather than cooking them too fast.

Keep boiled potatoes firm by adding a little vinegar to the boiling water. One part vinegar for every 2 parts water. Add a little salt too.

Making mash too? Use hot milk, which makes mashed potatoes lighter and fluffier.

For perfect mash, drop a teaspoon of sugar into the water as you boil the potatoes – it will make them more floury and they'll fluff up better.

Freshly grated horseradish will pep up mashed potato.

If your red cabbage turns blue or purple during boiling, add a tablespoon of vinegar to the water and the cabbage will turn red again.

When buying cabbage, check its bottom. If it's too white, don't buy it – it's a sign that the leaves and root have been trimmed off.

Cabbage can stink when it's being cooked. A bay leaf added to the boiling water will stop the smell without affecting the taste. Alternatively, reduce the cooking smells from cabbage water by adding a few caraway seeds to the pan.

To prevent an unpleasant odour when boiling cauliflower or cabbage, tear a slice of bread into small chunks and add it to the pot. The bread will absorb the smell. Rye bread works especially well.

Keep cauliflower white by adding 2 tablespoons of lemon juice or white wine vinegar to the cooking water.

Always buy broccoli with tight heads – this way they won't drop off when you cook them.

The stronger broccoli smells, the less fresh it is.

To stop broccoli smelling while cooking,

put a piece of red pepper in the pot with it while boiling.

Look out for really purple turnips – the more purple the turnip, the better it will taste.

When chopping up chilli peppers, avoid getting hot stuff on your skin by coating your hands with vegetable oil before handling them.

If your string beans have been around for a week and are starting to toughen, add some sugar to the water when cooking.

To check the quality of raw beans, put them in water. If they sink, they're good. If they float, throw them away.

If you have half an avocado left over, do not remove the stone, store it in the fridge – leaving the stone in will stop the flesh browning so quickly.

Store mushrooms in a paper bag to stop them sweating.

Carrots are easier to scrape if dunked in boiling water first.

Never store apples and carrots together because the apples give off a gas that makes the carrots go bitter.

And never store potatoes and onions together either. The potatoes will spoil faster.

A good artichoke will make a slight squeaking noise when handled.

If you find canned vegetables taste tinny, drain them, and then blanch in boiling water for one minute and rinse in cool water.

To cook delicious broad beans, add some chopped parsley to the water.

To stop onions from making you cry, burn a candle near by while chopping them. Alternatively, place a small piece of bread under your top lip – no more tears!

If your hands smell of onions, soak them in some milk.

There's no need to use a sticking plaster when you cut yourself. Press the inside of a clear onion skin on to the cut. Leave it there for as long as you can. Onion is a natural antiseptic.

If a recipe calls for 'finely chopped onions', just grate or blend some of them to save time.

To make onions brown more quickly when frying, add a pinch of sugar. They'll also taste delicious because they will be slightly caramelised.

To absorb the smell when frying onions, put a sheet of wet newspaper close to the hob.

Rice is one of the most common culinary disasters. Cook yours well in advance if you're having a dinner party or a special 'do'. Then, before it's quite done, turn off the heat. Leave the lid on and it will retain its heat while also losing some of its stodginess.

To stop rice sticking together, add a few drops of lemon juice to the boiling water.

Remember, rice triples its volume when cooked, so use a big enough pan.

To cook rice, soak in cold water for an hour or two first. This saves you time and fuel in the long run.

For bright white rice, squeeze some lemon juice into the water while boiling.

Add toasted nuts to rice while boiling to enhance the nuttiness.

Always fluff cooked rice with a fork – this allows the steam to escape and stops the grains from sticking together.

Cooked rice keeps well in the freezer, so make plenty and freeze the extra.

Never rinse your pasta – the starch helps the sauce stick to the pasta.

Raw spaghetti makes an excellent fire-lighter.

To check if your pasta is cooked, try flinging a piece against the oven door or the fridge. If it sticks, it's cooked.

Children love coloured pasta – add food colouring to the cooking water.

Salad Days

'I'm anorexic actually. An anorexic is someone who looks in the mirror and thinks they're fat. So do I.' *Jo Brand*

To keep salad really fresh, put a saucer upside down in the bottom of the bowl to collect any spare moisture.

To get the best from vinaigrette, make it at least an hour before dressing the salad to allow time for the flavours to mix together.

To dress a salad evenly, pour the dressing down the sides of the bowl rather than directly on to the salad.

Also try putting your dressing in a spray bottle to coat salad lightly. This usually saves calories, too.

To ripen tomatoes quickly, place them in a brown paper bag along with an already ripe tomato.

Don't store tomatoes in the fridge because they will blister.

If you do have to keep your tomatoes in the fridge, take them out a couple of hours before eating, as they become juicier at room temperature.

Soggy tomatoes will firm up if soaked in salty water for 10 minutes.

If you only need to use the tomatoes from the tin and not the juice, pour the leftover juice into an ice-cube tray for use in a gravy at a later date.

Make your lettuce last longer by cutting out the core and sprinkling sugar into the cavity.

To keep lettuce fresh for longer, wrap it in a paper towel, put it in a plastic bag and keep in the fridge.

If your lettuce has gone limp, put it in a bowl with a piece of rinsed coal and leave for several minutes.

Tear lettuce instead of cutting it to avoid the leaves turning brown.

To make celery that bit crisper, put it in a bowl of iced water and leave it in the fridge for a few hours.

Celery keeps longer if wrapped in foil.

It doesn't have to end in tears – store an onion in the fridge for several hours before using and you won't cry when you peel it.

If you want raw onions in your salad but

are worried that they will taste too strong, soak them in some tepid water first.

Raw carrots taste best if left in the fridge overnight in a pot of iced water with a little vinegar added to the water.

The more wrinkled a red pepper is, the sweeter and riper the taste.

Wrinkled green or yellow peppers aren't bad – they just have a mellower flavour.

Scoop out red or green peppers to make containers for mayonnaise, salad dressings, sauces and dips when entertaining.

Herb Lore

'There is no such thing as a little garlic.'
Arthur Baer

To keep watercress fresh for longer, immerse the leaves – but not the roots – in a jug of water.

To keep drinking water fresh, put a watercress leaf into a jug before filling with water and leave it there.

Make sure your parsley stays green – only add it to a sauce once the liquid has boiled.

To peel garlic easily, peel down the stem of the clove and soak in boiling water for a few minutes. The skin will then come straight off.

Freshen up bad breath instantly by chewing 2 or 3 sprigs of watercress and a couple of grapes.

To get rid of garlic breath, chew some parsley.

Freeze parsley on its stem in a clear plastic bag. When you need it, remove it from the freezer and rub it between your fingers. Your parsley is automatically chopped.

Keep fresh herbs longer – grind in a food processor, add 4 tablespoons of vegetable oil and refrigerate.

When a recipe calls for the leaf of a fresh herb to be added during cooking, add the stem of the herb instead. The stem has a stronger taste and, because it has less chlorophyll than the leaf, it won't add a green tint to the dish.

Remember, basil is one of the few herbs which increases in flavour when cooked so always add it at the end of cooking unless you want a really strong flavour.

Sage is the ideal herb to use with meat as it aids digestion of fat and its antiseptic qualities help to kill off any bugs in the meat as it cooks.

Always bruise a bouquet garni slightly with a mallet or rolling pin to release the aromatic oils before placing in your pot.

Chop mint the easy way – sprinkle some sugar on it first.

Put a bay leaf into stored flour to deter weevils.

Feeling Fruity

'The second day of a diet is easier than the first – by the second day you're off it.'
Jackie Gleason

When choosing lemons and oranges, always go for the fruit that feels too heavy for its size.

The smoother a lemon skin – the juicier the lemon.

To save money on lemons buy lots when they're on special offer. Squeeze the juice out and freeze it in ice-cube trays. When a recipe calls for lemon juice, just take out the required number of lemon ice cubes and add on the spot.

If you need to keep lemons fresh for a long time, store them covered in cold water.

Old, wrinkly lemons can be restored to their former glory by boiling them in water for a few minutes, then leaving to cool.

Before you grate citrus fruit, rinse the grater in cold water. After use, the peel will come away from the grater much more easily.

Also, to make peeling a grapefruit easier, pour boiling water over the fruit and leave to stand for 5 minutes.

For fruit salad with a difference, use lemonade instead of fruit juices. For a celebration, try champagne instead.

To chop dried fruit, wet the blade of the knife so the fruit doesn't stick to it.

Ripen green bananas by leaving a red tomato next to them.

To stop bananas from turning black in a fruit salad, cover the unpeeled fruit with cold water for 10 to 15 minutes before peeling.

Don't always buy with your eyes – the more crinkly the skin on a honeydew melon, the sweeter it will be inside.

To get more juice out of a citrus fruit, warm it in the oven for a few minutes before squeezing it. Alternatively, roll the fruit back and forth over a hard surface before cutting it in half.

Bounce your cranberries to find out if they are fresh or not. If they bounce, they are!

To trim gooseberries, use baby nail scissors.

To bring out the flavour of strawberries

when cooking them in desserts, add a touch of balsamic vinegar to the recipe.

To slice kiwis easily, just use an egg-slicer. Remove the skin of the kiwi by edging a teaspoon around the slice, between the flesh and the skin.

Keep fruit and veg longer by storing them in paper bags rather than plastic.

Perfect Puddings

'I wouldn't give somebody my last Rolo if they were in a diabetic coma.' *Jo Brand*

Keep cartons of double cream fresher for longer by turning the carton upside down in the fridge.

To make really light whipped cream, add a dash of icy-cold water just before you do the final whip.

If you get a little bit of yolk in the white when you are separating eggs, take a bit of tightly rolled kitchen towel that you have heated up in some boiling water and hold it near the yolk. The heat will draw the yolk towards the towel.

Eggs will stay fresher for longer if stored pointed end down.

To test whether an egg is fresh or not, hold it up to a burning candle. If there are black spots visible, the egg is bad.

To tell whether an egg is absolutely fresh, put it in a bowl of water. If it is really fresh, it will sink. Older eggs will float.

Egg whites thicken up faster when you add a pinch of salt before beating.

If your custard goes lumpy, quickly put the base of the pan into some cold water and keep whisking until things go smoothly again.

If custard 'scrambles' during cooking, put it in a liquidiser with a tablespoon of milk and spin it until it goes smooth again.

When making custard, gently heat the sugar in the pan before adding the milk – your custard will never boil over.

For a special custard for adults, pour in a small glassful of apricot or cherry brandy just before serving. Alternatively, add a measure of Bailey's Irish cream to custard for a really special flavour.

Before boiling milk, dampen the inside of the pan with water. When the milk boils, it won't burn the bottom.

If you are using baking recipes that call for liqueurs, buy a range of miniatures rather than invest in a whole bottle (you'll only be tempted to drink it!).

Treat adults to jelly made with a large dash of vodka. Enjoy experimenting with quantities at home. Make sure you don't get the children's and the adults' puddings mixed up.

Love double cream, but you're cutting down on calories? Evaporated skimmed milk makes an excellent substitute when slightly frozen.

Whipping cream calls for cool temperatures – refrigerate your utensils before you start.

Put ice-cream bowls in the fridge for 30 minutes before serving the ice cream – it won't melt so quickly.

For really simple frozen yogurt, put a lollipop stick into a carton of yogurt, freeze and remove the carton. Try different flavours and low-fat yogurts for a tasty slimming treat.

Dental floss pulled tightly will cut through cheesecake and other similar puddings with ease.

When making toffee, pour the mixture into greased ice-cube trays for ready-made bite-sized pieces.

When rolling pastry, put it between 2 sheets of cling film. You won't need to use extra flour to stop it sticking to the surfaces and it is easier to turn over, too.

A pinch of salt added to margarine makes whisking quicker.

Have a couple of small freezer bags ready when baking so that you can pop them over your floury hands if the phone rings.

Always let pie pastry dry thoroughly before adding the filling. A skin forms which prevents the filling from seeping in during cooking.

Put sugar in a pie, not on it. This gives a much more even flavour, and sugar on a pie often burns.

When slicing apples for pies, put the slices in water and add a little salt to stop them discolouring: it has the same effect as adding lemon but it's cheaper.

Store flour in the freezer to keep it for longer.

To stop the base and crust of fruit pies going soggy during cooking, sprinkle the pastry with flour before putting in the filling.

To stop pastry sticking to your rolling pin, put the pin in the freezer or fridge so that it's cold before you use it.

Save time when making biscuits – instead of cutting lots of individual round shapes, just roll the dough into a sausage and cut slices off it.

For really crispy biscuits, use half flour and half cornflour.

To make shortbread with that delicious luxury taste, add a tablespoon of custard powder to the raw mixture.

If you only have very cold butter to hand when baking, try grating it into a warm metal bowl. It will soon become softer and reach the right temperature.

To weigh golden syrup with minimal mess, just put the whole tin on the scales and keep spooning the sticky stuff out until the tin has gone down in weight by the amount you need.

To create an impressive chocolate bowl, brush or pipe lukewarm melted chocolate on to half of an inflated balloon until it's about 3 in/7.5 cm deep. Allow to cool thoroughly, then carefully burst the balloon.

If sugar goes hard and lumpy, pop it into your bread bin with a loaf and it will go soft.

To soften hard brown sugar, leave it in a bowl covered with a damp tea towel overnight. Alternatively, keep brown sugar soft by leaving a slice of apple in the jar.

To give your meringues a toffee flavour, use brown sugar.

A quick way to mark out squares for toffee or fudge is to press a wire cooling tray lightly on to a tin of the mixture. The grid marks left behind will be a clear guide to perfect little pieces.

To bring out the taste of chocolate in most recipes, add a few coffee granules.

Avoid mess and waste – cut the required amounts of frozen gateaux and cakes while they're still frozen.

To make individual pavlovas, drop the meringue mix on to the baking sheet in large dollops – they are lovely to serve at a dinner party and they also take less time to cook.

Melt your favourite chocolate bar in the microwave, then pour over ice cream for a delicious treat.

To make pretty chocolate curls, microwave a chocolate bar for 10 seconds and then use a cheese slice to create the curls.

Caramel sauces must not be allowed to boil. But if yours does, don't worry. Just stir in some milk or cream and turn it into toffee sauce.

To slice baked meringue easily, grease the knife with butter before cutting.

To make your mousses more decorative, make two: one with white chocolate and one with dark. Put each in a separate, small, piping bag. Then, put both bags in one large piping bag. Squeeze into a dish and, as the mousse comes out, it will be a beautiful swirl of the two colours. The taste combination of the sweet white chocolate and the bitter dark is lovely, too.

To get the best taste out of nuts in baking, toast them first on a baking tray before adding to the mix.

To prevent mould growing on the surface of jam, moisten the waxed circle on top of the jar with whisky.

To give a cake a wonderful golden glow, try adding custard powder to a basic sponge mixture.

When making cakes, leave the eggs and fat out overnight so that they will be at the same temperature.

If you don't have a cake tin with a removable base, don't worry. Grease your tin as normal. Cut a long strip of kitchen foil and put it into the bottom of the tin so that each end of the foil strip goes up the side and hangs over the edge. Put a circle of greaseproof paper in the bottom of the tin and fill with the cake mixture. When you need to get the cake out, gently lift it using the foil tabs.

Make sure any essence you use adds flavour to the whole cake – mix it into one of the eggs before adding to the mixture.

Your cakes will never stick if you use olive oil to grease the tins.

Before using a new baking tin, grease it and bake it in a very hot oven for at least 10 minutes. Wash as normal in soapy water and you'll find your tin stays as good as new for ages.

Do your cakes always sink? It's not necessarily the opening of the oven door that causes it but the closing. Unless you do it very gently, the sudden movement can cause the cake to sink.

Also, to help make sponge cakes rise, add a tablespoon of boiling water to the mix just before putting it in the tin.

If you want your cake to have a flat top for decorating, spoon out a bit of the mixture from the middle of the tin before baking.

To stop glacé cherries from sinking, coat them lightly in flour before using. Use the same treatment for nuts to prevent them from sinking to the bottom of the cake mix.

For an extra rich, tasty fruit cake use cold coffee instead of milk in your fruit cakes.

For a really moist fruit cake, use marmalade instead of candied peel.

Always soak dried fruit overnight – for extra flavour, soak the fruit in apple or orange juice.

If your cakes always come out cracked, put a dish of cold water in the bottom of the oven before baking.

To improve the flavour and texture of cakes and to reduce fat at the same time, substitute a third of the butter with a mashed banana.

To make fluffier, lighter cakes, whip the egg whites separately before adding to the recipe.

To make beating brown sugar into a cake mix easier, put it through a food processor first – it makes it softer.

For a moist fruit cake with extra flavour, grate a cooking apple into the mixture.

Before sandwiching your cake together with jam, spread a little butter on each sponge surface. This will stop the cake absorbing all the jam.

Use muslin instead of a sieve when dusting icing sugar through a doily. It is much finer and the effect is so much prettier.

Before icing a cake, sprinkle the top with some flour; this will stop the icing running down over the edges. For a deceptively clever effect, put two colours of icing in a bag and then pipe out. The two-tone effect is stunning.

If you don't have a turntable for decorating a cake, don't worry. Take two plates, sandwich them together back to back with a little cooking oil and place on a damp tea towel to stop the bottom plate slipping.

Placed on top, your cake will turn round beautifully.

Glacé icings can be horribly sweet. Substituting milk for some of the water gives a creamy texture and reduces the sweetness.

For a tasty, colourful cake topping, mix a little strawberry jam and boiling water into icing sugar.

Decorate your cakes with real flowers. To stop the flowers wilting cut a 3 in/7.5 cm piece of plastic drinking straw. Bend the end of the straw upwards and tape it. Fill the straw three-quarters full with water and insert the flower stem inside it.

Roll marzipan out between 2 sheets of cling film or aluminium foil.

To stop cake mix sticking to your spoon when you're transferring it to a tin, try dipping the spoon in milk beforehand.

Royal icing is notoriously difficult to beat with a food mixer. Try fixing the whisk attachment to a variable speed drill instead.

Leftover royal icing? Just add a little more icing sugar and a few drops of peppermint essence, then roll out and cut shapes to make peppermint creams.

Icing sets more quickly if made up with boiling water.

If you want beautiful, smooth icing on a cake, try using an artist's palette knife.

To prevent breaking icing when cutting a cake, dip the knife blade in boiling water first.

To fill an icing bag with no mess, put it inside a tall glass or a jug, fold the top of the bag over the rim, then fill.

To keep cakes fresh in the tin, throw in half an apple.

Say Cheese

To keep cheese fresh for longer, wrap it in a cloth that you have dampened with white wine vinegar.

A sugar cube in the cheese box will keep cheese fresh for longer.

Stop the sides of cheddar cheese going hard and waxy – spread a thin layer of butter over it before you wrap it up and put it away for the night.

Before serving cheese after a meal, warm the cheese knife in the oven. This makes it easier to cut through the cheese.

If you want perfect cheese curls, try using a potato peeler.

To prevent blocks of cheese going mouldy before you have the chance to use them, grate the cheese and freeze in a freezer bag.

To prevent yourself from cutting the ends of your fingers when grating cheese, wear thimbles.

To clean a cheese grater after grating the cheese, grate a raw potato. The potato will clear the cheesy gunk from the holes. Alternatively, to clean a grater, rub a hard crust of bread over it.

'A mother is a person who, seeing there are only four pieces of pie for five people, promptly announces she never did care for pie.' *Tenneva Jordan*

If you want the cream to float on your coffee rather than sink without trace, stir some sugar into the coffee first.

Add a touch of luxury to coffee with one teaspoon of vanilla ice cream instead of milk.

To bring out the taste of fresh coffee, put a pinch of dried mustard powder into the percolator.

To transform instant coffee into a more sophisticated offering, add a few cardamom seeds. Serve the coffee black . . . and remember to remove the seeds before serving!

Raise a Glass

'I never drink water – I'm afraid it will become habit-forming.' *W. C. Fields*

Wine will chill much quicker with the cork out – ideal if you're in a hurry for a cool glass of wine.

If you haven't got time to chill beer for your guests, just chill the glasses instead.

People often say they like dry white wine best but in blind tastings medium comes out on top. Choose medium for the safest bet at a dinner party.

All wines benefit from being decanted – even if you only use a simple jug.

If champagne starts to fizz over as you are pouring it, discreetly dip one of your fingers into the glass!

Keep the bubbles popping. Champagne bubbles go flat instantly if they come into contact with detergent so make sure your glasses are squeaky clean. Fill the glasses to the top so the bubbles last longer.

When you're pouring champagne, put a little in the bottom of each glass before topping them up. This stops them from over-flowing and wasting all the bubbly!

To keep champagne really fizzy, dangle a

teaspoon in the neck of the bottle.

Remember the 'designated drivers' and non-drinkers. Always have enough soft drinks. Try mixing fruit juice with mineral water rather than just having lots of fizzy drinks.

When freezing big bags of ice, sprinkle the cubes with some soda water to stop them all sticking together in lumps.

For a really fast chill, put wine (or beer) in an ice bucket and sprinkle salt (about 4 to 6 tablespoons) on to the ice.

Impress your guests with expensive wine first – then bring out the cheaper stuff when everyone's slightly merry and they'll hardly notice the difference.

To get the best from wine in sauces, put the wine in a pan and bring to the boil beforehand. Then set light to it with a match. The flame will burn off the alcohol and any sharpness. Add a touch of sugar to sweeten and then add to the sauce.

Fill an ice-cube tray with leftover wine to use in cooking at a later date.

It's messy when fizzy drinks overflow. To avoid this, pour fizzy drinks into warmed glasses and then put in lots of ice to chill the drink.

Keep your mineral water fizzy – give the

plastic bottle a good squeeze before screwing the top back on.

To frost a glass, put it in the freezer until a white, frosted look appears.

The best way to keep party punch cool is to freeze some of it in ice-cube trays or a ring mould. Float the frozen punch in the bowl to keep the rest of it chilled, but undiluted.

For very special party nibbles, inject cherry tomatoes with vodka and Worcestershire sauce – sprinkle with celery salt and black pepper for a very original take on the traditional Bloody Mary.

Flavoured vodka is all the rage in pubs and clubs so try making your own – cordials or crushed and puréed fruit can be added. Experiment with cordials lighter and heavier than the vodka itself for a pretty, layered drink.

Store fresh ginger in vodka – it will improve the taste of the vodka and the ginger.

To clean your decanter, half fill it with warm soapy water and 2 tablespoons of rice. Swish the mixture around and leave for half an hour before pouring out. Rinse the decanter and stand upside down to dry.

If the stopper gets stuck in a decanter, put a few drops of cooking oil around the neck and leave in a warm place for a while before loosening the stopper.

Prevent hangovers by eating a spoonful of coleslaw before bed (honest!). Alternatively, if you have had a bit too much to drink, have a slice of toast with honey before going to bed.

The Prairie Oyster is an ideal hangover cure. Rinse a glass with olive oil. Add tomato ketchup and a whole egg yolk. Season with Worcestershire sauce, vinegar, salt and pepper. Swallow the mixture in one gulp.

Feeling hung-over? Vitamin C is the most important ingredient in any hangover cure – soluble, flavoured vitamin tablets are virtually designed for hangovers. Alternatively, try tonic water at breakfast the morning after.

Keeping a Record

'The moment you have children yourself, you will forgive your parents everything.'
Susan Hill

Mother's Day party, christenings, birthdays . . . recording the family get-togethers over the years is important. Mums often end up as the official record keepers of the growing family. So make sure that you get the best out of your photographs.

Keep a record of the family. If you don't do it already, make sure you take a picture of the whole family at least once a year – why not on Mother's Day? Put them in a pretty album all of their own and watch the family change over the years.

Add a new look to photos – stand on a wall, as long as you are safe to do so. Getting up high changes the perspective and the nature of the shot completely – a trick that works wonders.

If you're taking photos with a timer, don't place the camera precariously on a wall. Half fill a plastic bag with pasta, shells, sand, scrunched-up newspaper or beans and put the camera on that. It makes a soft and manoeuvrable base for the camera to rest on.

If you have an important set of photos that you are afraid might get lost during the developing process, take a photo of your name and address on the first frame so that there is a record of who the photos belong to. Also, stick a label with your name and address on the film canister.

Don't bother to tell everyone to smile because the end result is bound to look forced. Instead, ask everyone to blow a rasp-berry. They'll feel so silly they'll end up laughing and you can then take a lovely natural shot. Blowing a raspberry also helps relax people's jaws and mouths where tension and nervousness can show most.

When taking a photograph of someone with a receding hairline, shoot from lower than eye level.

If your subject is an older woman, don't use a flash because it shows up the wrinkles . . . and she won't thank you for that!

Try shooting towards the sun but use a flash to fill in the face so you can see the features. Shooting at this angle means that your subject is nicely backlit.

If there's not enough light, ask someone wearing a white or pale shirt to stand close by so that you can bounce some light off them. Or you could ask someone to hold up a white handkerchief.

To take a shot of people on a sofa, put a telephone directory on the sofa for the person in the middle to sit on. Sofas tend to dip in the middle, leaving one person looking a lot shorter than everybody else.

When taking pictures of children, get down on their level so that they fill the frame.

To keep a small child happy while you take a photo, give them a piece of sticky tape to play with. They'll be amused for ages while you concentrate on getting some great shots.

'Be nice to your children. After all, they're going to choose your nursing home.' *Steven Wright*

To take a picture of a group of children, you want all of them looking at the camera at the same time . . . which can be difficult. Blow a whistle to get their attention and quickly take the picture.

To keep a camera still, get a piece of string and attach one end to your camera. Make a loop at the other end and hook it under your foot. This creates tension, which will help to steady the camera.

Say It with Flowers

With any luck, you will be inundated with flowers and plants by your grateful offspring. It's lovely to have flowers around you at any time of the year.

'One generation plants the trees; another gets the shade.' *Chinese proverb*

Flowers make a room – and a dining table – look great.

Don't worry about fancy arrangements. Handfuls – no, armfuls – of one kind of flower can look just as effective. Alternatively, use tiny vases, tea cups, glasses or jars to put just one or two striking blooms in.

You can group small flower-filled containers together for a clever effect.

Just put enough water in the vase to fill it between a third and a half full.

Use lukewarm water when arranging

flowers; it has less oxygen in it, so you don't get so many air bubbles up the stems of flowers.

Add a shot of vodka to the water in your vases – it will keep your flowers fresh for longer. Alternatively – if you want to keep the vodka for yourself – add a splash of lemonade to the water.

Keep the water fresh in your flower arrangement: drop a shiny copper penny into the bottom.

Use a spray of foxgloves to prolong the life of cut-flower arrangements. Alternatively, you can make an infusion of foxglove leaves and flowers by pouring water on them and leaving overnight. Add this water to your vase of flowers the next day.

When arranging flowers, strip off all leaves below the waterline to prevent them rotting.

Smash hard, woody stems but cut soft stems before placing them in your arrange-ment.

Perk up woody-stemmed flowers (such as roses) by putting the stems in boiling water for ten seconds, and then immediately plung-ing them into deep, cold water. This will move the air lock that has formed in the stem up to the flower.

If your flower arrangement is going to be

in a warm room, keep the blooms looking lovely by popping some ice cubes into the water each morning.

Revive droopy tulips and roses – wrap them tightly in wet newspaper and put them in a deep bucket of water overnight. Alternatively, revive droopy flowers by putting a soluble aspirin in the vase water – it's a great pick-me-up for them.

Don't put flowers next to fruit because the fruit produces ethylene gas, which increases the maturity rate of flowers, so they die more quickly. Equally, remove dying flowers from a bunch or arrangement because they produce the same gas.

Also, don't place flowers in direct sunlight, near central heating or on top of the television. Make sure they are in a well-ventilated part of the room.

Scented flowers don't last as long as non-scented varieties because they use up extra energy creating the smell.

Don't mix daffodils with other blooms – they release a poison that kills off other flowers.

Cut wide-stemmed flowers under water and then, keeping your finger over the cut end to stop air from getting into the stem, transfer to the vase.

Cut poppies will loose sap quickly and

therefore won't last long unless you carefully singe the ends in a candle flame to create a seal.

Remove the stamens from lilies to prevent the pollen from staining clothes and furnishing fabrics. Wipe up any pollen that falls on to polished wood surfaces because, if left, it will eat into the wood.

If the pollen from flowers has fallen on to your carpet or furnishing fabrics, lift it off gently with sticky tape so that you don't rub it in and leave an indelible stain.

Sharpen scissors by cutting tin foil.

To keep your posy of roses fresh, punch holes in a raw potato and insert each stem into a hole separately. Your flowers will stay fresh and pretty for a considerable time.

A pinch of salt or sugar in a flower arrangement slows down bacterial growth.

To keep fresh tulips closed, paint them with unbeaten egg white.

When arranging flowers with soft stems, make a hole for the stem in the oasis using a knitting needle.

Store oasis in a bucket of water – it should never be allowed to dry out.

If you don't have any oasis, put sticky tape across the top of the vase in a criss-cross pattern to form a grid to hold the flowers upright.

Use pebbles from the garden (make sure they are clean first) instead of oasis in the bottom of the vase.

Marbles hold flowers in place. If used in a glass vase, they look attractive, too.

To make flower arranging easy, put a wire scouring pad in the bottom of the vase and push the flower stems into the wire. The pad will last longer than oasis and, unlike oasis, can be used again even after it dries out.

Use polystyrene for drainage instead of stones.

If your vase has a small crack in it, seal the leak with a piece of soft candle wax.

If your vase is too big for the number of flowers you have, put a smaller tumbler inside the vase, fill it with water and put the flowers in that. The flowers will stand upright in the vase and won't look overwhelmed or droopy.

Clean vases regularly with bleach – not washing-up liquid – to kill the bacterial residue. Flowers are dirty things!

To clean a smelly vase, half fill it with water and add a tablespoon of mustard. Shake the mixture and then leave for an hour.

Cut flowers in the late evening and they'll last longer.

When looking at a plant, there's nothing wrong with taking the plant out of its pot and checking its root system.

Avoid plants that have moss, algae or weeds growing in their compost. This could mean that the plant has been in its pot too long.

Preserve dried flowers by spraying with hairspray. It acts like an adhesive and prevents them from falling apart.

Revitalise dried roses by holding them over a kettle of boiling water.

Home, Sweet Home

'When they come up with a riding vacuum cleaner, then I'll clean the house.'
Roseanne Barr

Well, you wouldn't be a mum if you didn't have one eye on wiping up messes, keeping the house clean and putting the pieces back together again once your little darlings have swept through like a whirl-wind. Here are a few hints and tips to make this part of being a mum that little bit easier.

When light bulbs are cool, dab on some of your favourite perfume. When the light is on and the bulb heats up, the room will be filled with the aroma.

To get rid of rings or minor scratches on wood, cover with petroleum jelly and leave for 24 hours. Rub it into the wood, wipe off the excess and then polish as normal.

Polish wood with metal polish instead of the normal woody kind and it should come up a treat.

To remove a scratch from a table, crack open a walnut and rub it along the scratch. Walnuts contain a natural resin that will conceal the scratch.

To remove greasy stains from wood, mix talcum powder and methylated spirits into a sloppy paste. Paint on to the stain and leave to dry. Brush off.

To get rid of ink stains from furniture, soak a piece of cotton wool in water and cover the stain with it. The mark will be drawn out and into the cotton wool.

Also, to remove ink stains from all sorts of materials, spray with hairspray first and then clean.

To keep silver clean, use lemon and salt.

Remove wax easily from silver candlesticks. Place them in the fridge overnight and it's then easy to pick off the wax.

Prevent tarnish by storing silver wrapped in cling film.

Scratches in glassware will disappear if polished with toothpaste.

To stop stairs and floorboards from squeaking – use a wax-based furniture polish.

You can raise dents in wood by placing a damp cloth over the dent and holding a warm iron (don't get it too hot) over the cloth for a few minutes. The moisture from the cloth swells the grain. Allow the wood to dry before polishing.

Repair a dent in wood by filling with a few drops of clear nail varnish.

Furniture can leave dents in the carpet. A cube of ice left on the dent will restore the pile of the carpet. Or, raise dents in carpets made by heavy furniture by rubbing the dent with the edge of a coin. Alternatively, remove dents in carpet pile by covering with a damp cloth and then quickly placing a hot iron on top. The steam lifts the pile.

If you need to fill a small hole in a wall in an emergency, use some toothpaste. Let it dry before painting the wall.

Wipe large items like freezers and washing machines with car wax to make them shine and to remove small scratches.

If your freezer is kept in the garage, polish the outside of the cabinet with car wax. This prevents its being affected by damp, mould or rust.

'No woman has ever shot her husband while he was doing the dishes.' *George Coote*

To clean burnt saucepans, soak them in Coca-Cola for a while. Alternatively, boil up some sliced onions and water in the pan and leave for several hours. Or, boil up some water and vinegar in the burnt pan and leave overnight. It will be easier to clean in the morning.

To clean really baked-in food from a cooking pan, put a sheet of fabric conditioner in the pan and fill with water. Leave overnight and the next day the food will just lift off with a sponge.

If you have a discoloured aluminium pan, boil up a weak solution of rhubarb or tomatoes in it. The food acids lift the stain. Alternatively, boil apple peel in a little water. This will make the aluminium pan much easier to clean afterwards.

To clean a rusty knife, plunge it into an onion and leave it there for half an hour. Wash and then polish it lightly with some vegetable oil.

If you've dropped a glass, use a piece of white bread to 'blot' up the tiny slivers of glass.

Dropped an egg on the kitchen floor?
Add some salt to the egg, leave it for 5
minutes and it will clean up more easily.

**To remove strong food smells from
plastic chopping boards**, give them a rub
down with a cut grapefruit.

After washing your baking trays, put them
back in the oven while it's still warm to
prevent them from going rusty.

**When you're cooking from a recipe
book**, cover the open page with some cling
film to stop it getting marked.

For a truly sweet-smelling fridge, pour
vanilla extract on to a piece of cotton wool
and leave it on one of the shelves inside.

To clean your dishwasher, simply run a
cup of white vinegar through the entire cycle
of the empty dishwasher.

**To get rid of odours from plastic contain-
ers**, fill with crumpled black-and-white
newspaper. Cover tightly and leave overnight.
Next day the smell is gone.

**Keep your waste disposal unit smelling
sweet** by grinding citrus rind (orange, lemon
or lime). Or use the discarded baking soda
after it has finished absorbing odours in the
refrigerator.

**If your waste disposal still has bad
breath**, try feeding it a handful of ice cubes,

a splash of vinegar, a lemon and a pinch of allspice.

To give a stainless-steel sink a superb finish, rub it down with a scrunched-up ball of newspaper after cleaning.

For a sparkling white sink, bleach is best. But it is expensive to fill a sink with bleach. Instead, line it first with kitchen paper then soak the paper in bleach. Leave for an hour or so before throwing the paper away.

'Everybody wants to save the earth ... nobody wants to help Mom do the dishes.'
P. J. O'Rourke

To clean the microwave, place half a lemon in a bowl of water and boil in the microwave for a few minutes. The lemony steam will vaporise all those greasy stains and clear nasty smells.

To clean up any spills in the oven, sprinkle some salt and cinnamon over the spill. This stops the house from filling with that acrid smoke smell and the spill will be easy to lift off with a spatula. Alternatively, sprinkle the spill with automatic dishwashing powder, cover with a wet paper towel and let it stand for a few hours, then clean with a damp sponge.

Messy ovens needn't take hours to clean. A sheet of aluminium foil on the bottom will catch all the drips and spills. Replace as necessary.

Wipe one side of the window horizontally and the other vertically. That way you will know which side the smears are on.

Make sure dirt stays in the dustpan – spray the inside with furniture polish so the dust has something to stick to.

A room will smell clean and polished when you spray furniture polish behind the radiator. The heat will disperse the smell around the room.

A terry nappy is good for wiping cornices because the loops get into all the detail.

For chrome taps or fixtures, try rubbing them with alcohol for a super shine.

Dripping taps can cause stains on the bath or sink enamel. Try rubbing the mark with a cut lemon to get rid of it.

If your acrylic bath gets scratched, try rubbing the scratches with silver polish.

Wipe bathroom mirrors with some washing-up liquid on a cloth – this will reduce condensation.

To descale tap nozzles, put a plastic bag filled with vinegar over the nozzle. Secure it with an elastic band and leave it for at least half an hour.

To clean glass shower doors, try using left-over white wine.

Glass shower doors will stay cleaner longer if you spray them lightly with furniture polish and then shine.

To stop the bottom of your shower curtain from becoming discoloured or mouldy, coat it with baby oil.

Chrome taps come up a treat if you rub them with some plain flour, then wash off.

'The best way to get a husband to do anything is to suggest he is too old to do it.'
Shirley MacLaine

To clean a toilet bowl, pour a can of Coca-Cola around the rim. Leave it for an hour and then brush and flush. Alternatively, drop several denture-cleaning tablets into the toilet bowl.

Prevent the bottom of a bathroom pull cord getting discoloured – place the casing from a clear ballpoint pen over the 'pulling' end.

To remove a cigarette singe mark from a carpet, pour a little milk on the stain and leave it to soak in. This will dilute the colour and stop it browning. Then rub the stain with a raw potato and wash as normal.

To clean wallpaper, use stale but still slightly moist bread. This gets the marks off without the need for soap and water.

To get rid of dog or cat hair on furniture,

use a damp rubber glove. Alternatively, collect cat or dog hairs from furniture with a fabric-conditioner sheet.

To clean silk flowers, put them into a large paper bag with a generous scoop of salt. Shake vigorously until all the dust is removed from the flowers.

To remove difficult, dried-on stains, sew a button on to the corner of the cloth you use for wiping down surfaces. Use the edge of the button to scrape off any stubborn, crusty stains you come across.

Changing duvet covers needn't end up as a wrestling match. Put one corner of the duvet into its cover and hold it in position with a clothes peg. Repeat with the other corner and shake the duvet down into the cover.

Put some washing-up liquid in the children's paints – it helps to get the paint out of clothes when they're being washed.

Keep new trainers looking white for longer – spray them with starch when you get them home from the shops. This makes them easier to clean as well.

To clean white training shoes rub with bathroom cleaner, buff and then wipe off with a rag. Alternatively, use cheap face-cleansing milk.

On Being a Mum

'I want to have children but my friends scare me. One of them told me she was in labour for thirty-six hours. I don't even want to do something that feels good for thirty-six hours.' *Rita Rudner*

Once labour starts, avoid getting to hospital too early. When contractions begin, try setting yourself a little task to finish before you leave. Tidying a drawer or writing a letter not only kills time but will also help to distract you from the discomfort of early labour.

To help you relax and prepare you for labour, try running a warm bath. You'll enjoy it far more at home than in a hospital bathroom.

Labour has been compared to running a marathon. Prepare yourself for the big event by eating lots of carbohydrates – potatoes, pasta, bread and vegetables.

Many women can't face eating or drinking during labour. Your mouth gets very dry so take a damp sponge to suck on for when you get dry.

Back pain can be a real problem in labour. Try making a simple back rub by filling a sock with some uncooked rice mixed in with a little massage oil, and knotting the open end. When you need it, ask the midwife to pop the sock in the microwave (most hospitals have them) and then get your partner or anyone else who's with you to rub it over the painful part of your back.

To help ease back pain, take the weight off your spine – kneel on all fours with your bottom in the air and your head on a pillow. Perhaps not the most flattering position you'll ever find yourself in, but at this point, who cares? For sheer reassurance and comfort, take a hot-water bottle with you into hospital.

Women in labour often get very hot – ask your partner or someone else with you to have a plant spray filled with cool water to hand so you can have a quick burst of cool spray when things start to heat up.

If you have long hair, take a hairband. There's nothing worse when you're hot and sticky than having your hair flop all over your face.

'A baby is God's opinion that the world should go on.' *Carl Sandburg*

After the birth you are likely to be starving. Be prepared and have some high-energy food ready, such as a chocolate bar or a banana.

Soothe sore stitches with a bag of frozen peas wrapped in a soft cloth.

To speed up healing after stitches, add some salt to the bath or, even better, some good-quality lavender oil.

Drying with a towel can be painful, but it's important to keep stitches clean and dry. Try a quick blast with the hair dryer.

Weeing can really sting if you've had stitches. When nature calls, try standing up in a cool shower – the running water will dilute the acid that causes the burning sensation.

Having stitches makes it painful to sit down. Try sitting on a child's rubber ring – you may feel a little silly but it's a great way to reduce painful pressure on the sore area.

To stop your breasts feeling sore, pop a couple of cabbage leaves inside your bra.

For sore boobs, make up a camomile poultice. Put 2 tablespoons of camomile flowers into a mug of boiling water and leave it to stand for about 10 minutes. Check the temperature is not too hot, and then soak a flannel in the camomile tea and hold it gently on the affected area. Leave until the flannel has cooled.

If your nipples are sore from breastfeeding, you can put on some marigold ointment but you should wipe it off carefully before feeding your baby.

Go to the doctor if you get sudden pains, a rash or feel as if you're coming down with flu. It could be mastitis, which must be treated straight away.

Prepare a thermos so that you can have a nice warm drink while you do the feed in the middle of the night.

'As a breastfeeding mother you are basically meals on heels.' *Kathy Lette*

Lots of new mums suffer hair loss. Add some powdered gelatine to your shampoo and leave it on for 10 minutes to encourage the return of glossy locks.

Start building up a mental map of where all the mother-and-baby rooms are in your area so that you won't panic if you get caught short.

Remember what we said right at the beginning of this book. Try to make some time for yourself. When the baby is asleep or someone is looking after it for you, try to do something that you enjoy – read a magazine, have a hot soak, listen to some music.

Be kind to yourself after the birth. Don't go on a strict diet – you will be tired and need all the energy you can get. There isn't a prize for getting back into your jeans within a fort-night.

'There was never a child so lovely, but his mother was glad to get him asleep.' *Ralph Waldo Emerson*

Your new bundle of joy will cry more than you think. Don't worry. The average baby will cry for at least two hours a day, and up to four is not unusual. If you accept it's normal, you'll find it less stressful.

Newborn babies may appear to be very fragile but will be much happier if you handle them firmly – they're used to being contained in a very confined space so try wrapping them quite firmly in a blanket.

Babies are born without any bacteria in their mouths. Nearly all children under three catch tooth-decaying germs from their mother's saliva, so avoid 'cleaning' your baby's dummy or teething ring by sucking on it yourself.

If your baby gets colic, try lying him face down across your lap with his tummy resting on a hot-water bottle filled with warm water.

Babies hate having tight things pulled over their heads so choose clothes with wide, envelope necks.

However pretty they may be (the clothes, not the baby!), don't choose knitwear with lacy patterns. Babies will only get their fingers caught up in them.

Jaundice is common in babies. Lying in natural sunlight for a short time, while adequately dressed to avoid either cold or sunburn, clears it up quickly.

When bottle-feeding your baby, you must keep the bottle at such an angle that the teat is always full of milk. Swallowing air while feeding is the most common cause of colic.

You can get pregnant when breast-feeding – most accidental pregnancies happen within nine months of giving birth! So perhaps we should learn from the women of Papua New Guinea who abstain from having sex until their firstborn can walk, or the African Masai who don't have sex again until the little one has cut its teeth!

Don't be too fastidious about constantly washing and changing the cot sheets – babies like the smell of familiar surroundings.

To reassure a baby and encourage good sleeping habits, place something in the cot that the baby's mum has worn during the day.

Leave a babysitter an item of clothing belonging to either parent to wrap the baby in if he wakes up feeling fretful.

Leave a babysitter a tape of Mum or Dad singing or, for older children, telling a story.

Don't hush everything up when you put your baby to sleep. Teach your child to sleep through normal noise levels.

'It is not advisable to put your head around your child's door to see if it is asleep . . . it was.' *Faith Hines*

Young babies don't need expensive toys. They will love to watch a washing machine going round or listen to a vacuum cleaner. Many new mothers try to keep all noises down – but babies find them fascinating and it's good to get them used to normal domestic surroundings.

Bathing tiny babies can be a bit tricky. You may find it easier to bathe them in a baby bath rather than bending down over a large tub.

If your baby dislikes having a bath, it may be because the bathroom is too cold. Make sure the room is warm before you start the bath, or bathe the baby in another, warmer room.

To prevent babies from slipping in a big bath, use a terry nappy as a non-slip mat.

Never leave a baby or child alone in the bath. It only takes a few inches of water for a child to drown so always supervise them.

Babies quickly get cold after a bath. Make sure you have everything you'll need before you put your baby in the water.

Feed your baby after his bath and not before. Babies often decide to throw up if they've been jiggled around, so wait until after they've been cleaned before feeding.

'You can learn many things from children. How much patience you have, for instance.' *Franklin P. Jones*

Use plastic stacking boxes from DIY stores for storage. They are cheaper than specially designed baby equipment.

When babies are young, put them in nighties rather than playsuits at night. It will make night changes easier and less disruptive, and begin to teach them the difference between night and day.

Lay out a clean set of night clothes before you go to bed so that you're not stumbling around in the dark if you have to do a complete change in the wee small hours.

Make your own baby wipes – they're cheaper and less synthetic. Simply soak some cotton-wool roll in an old ice-cream carton filled with water and a little baby oil. Tear off strips as you need it.

Make your own nappy-rash cream. Whip up an egg white until it has soft peaks. Apply it to the affected area with cotton wool.

Cradle cap looks horrid – a little almond oil should clear it up in no time.

Teething can be a major problem. Cut some slightly stale bread into fingers, dip into milk and then bake for a couple of minutes until brown for excellent teething strips.

To soothe hot, painful gums, put some fresh fruit flesh into the middle of a muslin square and twist the cloth into a tight sausage. Chill it in the fridge for a couple of hours then let your baby gnash away at it.

Always have lots of muslin squares around – they have lots of uses. Try placing one over a pillow to save laundry if your baby keeps posseting; or use one tied to the cot with a little vapour rub on it to help a sniffly baby. Take the chill off a baby-changing mat by laying a muslin square across it first.

Cleaning first milk teeth is a fiddly job and many babies hate toothbrushes. Instead, wrap a little muslin around your finger – it makes it much easier to get at little gnashers.

To wind a baby, try holding him or her over your shoulder and walk up and down the stairs – the natural up-and-down movement works much better than trying to bounce the baby and the rhythm is relaxing, too.

'Wealth and children are the adornment of life.' *Koran*

When you first wean a baby on to solids, you will only need a bit each time. Avoid waste and make life more convenient by making up large batches of fresh vegetables or fruit then puréeing them into ice trays to use as needed.

Introduce new foods one after the other. You can then detect more easily if your child is allergic to anything.

Save time by cooking for the whole family at once. Cook the 'grown-up' food without seasoning, put a little to one side for your baby and purée it. Then season your own food the way you like it.

Don't use baby talk. It doesn't help children to pick up anything useful. Use simple, short sentences and look at children when you speak to them.

Expand on what your child says. Always try to add new words for your child to learn. If they point out a fire engine in the street, you can say, 'Yes, it's a red fire engine'.

When you wash children's hair, draw a thin line of petroleum jelly above their brow; it will stop the shampoo running down into their eyes and stinging them. Alternatively, get them to wear a golf visor.

To cure an early riser, try setting an alarm clock! It may sound mad, but children love gimmicks and your toddler will start to wait for the bell to go off, often falling asleep again before that time comes. Eventually, their body clock will change, teaching them to sleep until your chosen time of waking.

Keep the route from the nursery to your room clear of obstacles. If your child comes looking for you at night, you don't want them tripping over things in the dark. And put up a safety gate at the top of the stairs.

If your child is suffering from nightmares, make a point of turning the pillow over to 'turn the bad dreams away'. Leave a night light or soft light on in the room.

Encourage toddlers to dress themselves by laying out their clothes so they can see the whole outfit. Then make the task a game by setting a clock and challenging them to a race against time.

Teach little ones their left and right by putting stickers on their wellies.

To teach children to tie their shoelaces, get some liquorice laces and practise making edible butterflies.

'Any mother could perform the job of several air traffic controllers with ease.' *Lisa Alther*

When children want to start feeding themselves, dress them in a painting bib rather than a normal feeding bib – it will cover much more of their clothing and is waterproof so can be wiped clean.

Faddy eaters may be encouraged to eat if you make mealtimes fun. Arrange food to create patterns or to spell out their name.

Involve toddlers in buying food and cooking – they'll feel much more inclined to taste something they've helped to prepare.

Arrange finger foods in the different compartments of an ice-cube tray – children love 'little things'.

A fun way to encourage children to eat their dinner is to give them chopsticks instead of knives and forks (not for the faint-hearted or anyone with a new carpet).

For a healthy and tasty pizza with a difference, spread some Marmite on to a pizza base before adding favourite toppings.

To create fun-shaped sandwiches for children, use metal pastry cutters.

Children thrive on routine in their daily activities. Try to serve meals at the same time each day.

Snacks are not always bad for children. Nutritious snack foods can help children to get the required nutrients. Since children have smaller stomachs than adults, they are natural grazers – so serving three small meals with a nourishing snack in between each meal may be more appropriate than serving three large meals.

Children's appetites may suddenly decrease around the age of two due to a decrease in their growth rate. As growth slows, energy requirements are also reduced. So don't worry if a previously hungry hippo turns into a nibbling mouse.

Don't present children with huge helpings – they'll eat much better if confronted with an obviously manageable portion and, if they then manage a second helping, they'll feel a real sense of achievement.

For an easy snack slice frankfurters into 4 strips lengthways and then cut into small pieces that can't block the windpipe and cause the child to choke.

Cook meat at a low temperature (150–160°C/300–325°F/gas 2–3) to keep it tender and juicy.

When children are first learning to feed themselves, cut meat into small julienne strips that can be picked up and eaten by hand. Older children who are using tableware still need to have their meat cut into bite-sized pieces with the fat and gristle trimmed to prevent choking.

Children usually enjoy brightly coloured fruits and vegetables.

Children like their vegetables crunchy, not soft. Vegetables steamed in a small amount of water, microwaved or stir-fried are not only crisp, but retain most of their colour, flavour and nutrients far better than boiled ones.

Many strongly flavoured vegetables such as cabbage, turnip, cauliflower, spinach, broccoli and asparagus are very acceptable to children when served with grated cheese or a cheese sauce.

To prevent choking, avoid giving raw carrots and whole peas, corn and grapes to children under 4 years old. Cook and mash carrots, corn and peas, and cut grapes into quarters.

Many older children enjoy raw vegetables served with their own individual bowl of dip.

When shopping with children, encourage them to help select fruits and vegetables, especially ones they have never tried before.

Cover the floor directly beneath a child's seat with paper, vinyl or plastic.

Place food at the level of a child's stomach, where it is less tiring for a child to reach.

Sometimes children behave better and enjoy mealtimes more when they sit down to a meal with the family at a nicely set table. Allowing older children to have candles makes a meal into a special occasion, and little ones can help to blow them out when everyone's eaten well. But remember, never leave children alone with candles that are alight.

Encourage children to try at least one bite of a new food. If, after one bite, children reject it, reintroduce the food later.

Start nutrition education early by explaining the function of nutrients found in common foods (for example that milk makes bones and teeth strong).

Encourage children to participate in quiet activities before mealtimes. It's difficult to get an excited child to settle down to eat.

Children's blood sugar levels often run low quite quickly. If your toddler suddenly seems irritable for no apparent reason, try giving him a little bit of fruit or cheese.

Boring bites can be transformed into magical meals with a few drops of food colouring and a little imagination. Mashed potato can become green grass or blue sea, pasta can be colourful snakes, and rice can be any colour of the rainbow. Even the humble egg boiled in its shell can become jewel red or sunshine yellow. Choose your child's favourite colour and they'll soon start eating up.

Whenever eating, children should be sitting upright, not lying down or running around. Always supervise at snack and mealtimes, because a child who is choking cannot make a noise to attract your attention. Coughing, on the other hand, is a sign that the child is removing the obstacle naturally. Before intervening, give the child the chance to cough out the food.

When travelling by car, bus or train with young children, consider their needs. Pack snacks when taking a trip that will last longer than one hour.

Pay attention to the special needs of children when dining with them at restaurants. If you must wait before being seated, take children for a walk outside the restaurant to prevent them from becoming impatient.

Some children expect to eat as soon as they sit at a dinner table and will fill up on appetisers and bread, leaving no room for their main meal. Try to prevent this by asking the restaurant not to put out the bread in advance of the meal and, when you order, enquire about children's portions.

Children involved in meal preparation develop a more active interest in food. They can accomplish many different tasks when working one-on-one with an adult in the kitchen. A number of activities children can do successfully at various ages are listed below. Having patience and time to spend with children when involving them in meal preparation is the key to success:

- *Two- and three-year-olds* need to learn about personal hygiene – encourage them to wash their hands before handling any food or eating.
- *And they love having 'jobs' to do.* Try asking them to wash vegetables, wipe the table, tear lettuce, help to shape burgers and meatballs, peel bananas (if the top is started) and clear their own place setting.
- *Three- and four-year-olds* like to feel challenged. Let them break eggs into a bowl, measure and mix ingredients, knead and shape dough, pour their own cereal out and toss salads.
- *Five-year-olds* can make cakes and cookies using baking mixes, help make pancakes, French toast, scrambled eggs, hot cereal and rice (with close supervision), set and clear the table and load the dishwasher.
- *Encourage teenagers to help out in the*

kitchen. Put up a notice each day saying what's for dinner. If they get home before you they will know which vegetables to start chopping or to preheat the oven. You may even find dinner waiting for you – but don't bank on it!

'The best way to keep children at home is to make the home atmosphere pleasant – and let the air out of the tyres.'
Dorothy Parker

For healthy ice lollies that will still please little ones, top and tail a pineapple and cut downwards into 6 to 8 chunky wedges, then freeze.

Give the kids a treat with homemade creamy banana ice lollies. Blend a banana with some milk, then pour into moulds, add a stick and freeze.

When making your own ice lollies, put any piece of real fruit in to pep up the taste and make them healthy.

Keep insects out of the children's drinks when having a picnic. Cover the tops of beakers with cling film and push a straw through.

Children will love bananas if you coat them in melted chocolate and roll them in coconut.

Dilute pure fruit juice with sparkling mineral water when serving to children.

Do your kids' hands get messy when eating ice lollies? Just take a disc of card, put the stick of the lolly through the card and, as the lolly melts, the juices will just drip on to the card and not on to the child's hands.

For fun cup cakes, top them with a marsh-mallow a couple of minutes before removing from the oven.

Children don't usually like ice-cold milk – try pouring it a short time before serving to take off the chill.

If children refuse to drink milk, try to include milk-based soups, cottage cheese, yogurt, cheese, custard or cereal with milk in their diets.

Young children often prefer the taste of bland, sweet fruits over tart fruits. Serve tart fruits from time to time to develop a child's taste for all fruits.

Do not offer sweets as a bribe or withhold them as punishment.

Since children know that sweets exist, serving sweets on special occasions may be a more sensible approach than excluding them completely. By sometimes including them in your child's diet, you avoid making them into a big deal.

'It is not a bad thing that children should occasionally, and politely, put parents in

their place.' *Colette*

Children love sweets but to keep things under control put the sweets in the freezer for a couple of hours. The paper should peel off easily and the sweets won't be too sticky for little fingers.

Tantrums and the 'terrible twos' needn't be the end of your sanity. They are just a cry for attention. If you ignore them, the toddler will realise they don't work. If your child is really stubborn, try leaving the room yourself and say 'I don't want to be with you while you do that' – young children hate to be ignored and will soon come and say sorry!

To cut children's hair without tears or mistakes, trim the ends while they're asleep.

If cutting children's hair, try putting them in front of a fish tank – or something that holds their attention. Alternatively, draw a blank face on a piece of paper. As you cut your child's hair, get them to stick the cut pieces around the face on the paper.

Dressing up can be great therapy for shyness and can be used to overcome fears. Superman wouldn't be scared of the dentist and Cinderella would always have clean teeth and hair!

When children are cleaning their teeth, use an egg timer in the bathroom so they know how long they should clean their teeth for.

To wean a toddler off a dummy, have a special box that is home for the offending pacifier. At night, after the child falls asleep, put the dummy in the box – letting the child know it is there if it is needed. At some stage, send the box off to Father Christmas or the fairies, then return it to the child with a small toy in it instead of the dummy.

Children love magic and surprises. Make special paper by writing messages or the children's names in white crayon on white paper. When they colour the paper in, they'll reveal your message.

Make modelling dough out of flour, water and some food colouring. Children enjoy the process of making it as much as the modelling that follows and it's much cheaper than buying it ready-made. If your child makes something really good, this homemade recipe can be baked hard and kept afterwards.

Use old offcuts of wallpaper and get your child to lie down on the plain side. Draw around them to make a silhouette and then pin it up and get them to colour it in with whatever they fancy.

To make a fun place-mat for your child, take one of their paintings and stick it on to a cork table mat. Then cover the mat with some clear sticky-back plastic.

Use sponges and vegetables as stamps. Cut out a simple design for them and then leave them to make patterns on paper by dipping the stamp in paint.

If your children have made thickly daubed finger paintings, a quick blast of hairspray will stop the bits of paint falling off once it's dried.

Keep a box of odds and ends that you can use for drawing, sticking things together or modelling. Old toothbrushes, old office stationery, large buttons, yogurt pots, cereal packets and that old standby the washing-up bottle! Keep everything in shoe boxes for a rainy day.

Encourage your children to tidy their rooms with an egg timer or clock. Make it a race with prizes for the tidiest competitor.

Teach young children to count by marking the back of a jigsaw in numerical order. The little ones can enjoy piecing the jigsaw together using the numbers as a guide and then turn it over to see the finished picture. The numbers will also help you to quickly check if you have all the pieces.

It's important to calm children down at the end of the day. Read them stories and let them know that the quieter they are, the longer you'll read. If they start being noisy, it's end of story.

Children's tattoos don't always come off easily – use a tiny drop of nail-polish remover on a cotton bud.

'The main purpose of children's parties is to remind you that there are worse children than your own.' *Katherine Whitehorn*

Children's parties needn't be a night-mare for parents. Don't do too much food: children are often too excited to eat a lot. Make sure you've moved all your precious objects out of harm's way. If all the children are under four, they'll need one-to-one super-vision. If children are four or five years old, it's best to have one adult for every five chil-dren.

Themed parties always go down well. Pirates, cowboys, spacemen are just a few popular ideas. Don't be too ambitious though, or you'll find nobody will turn up in costume.

Hire a large-screen projector from a camera shop and rent a video from your local video store.

Be imaginative when making invitations – use white paper plates, photographs or folded paper shapes, for example.

Save your puff! Balloons are easier to blow up if soaked in water first.

If you have more than 10 children attending, split pass the parcel into 2 groups.

Make a fun jail – get some plywood and a couple of old sheets. Paint bars on to the sheets and use it as a 'detention centre'.

Party bags are expensive. Why not give all the children one present as they leave. A football or decent yo-yo and perhaps a balloon can work out cheaper than a bag of nonsense. Alternatively, have a lucky dip at the door as children leave. To make a lucky dip, go to a pound shop and buy as many gifts as you want. Ask the children to decorate the lucky dip box while you wrap the presents. If you've got things that are particularly for girls or boys, colour-code the wrapping to avoid tantrums.

If you don't have enough room to play musical chairs, play musical hats instead.

Children love personalised games so get each of the parents to bring a baby photo of their child. The game is to recognise who the baby is in each photo.

Personalise 'pin the tail on the donkey'. Photocopy and enlarge a photo of the birthday girl or boy for the children to pin a red nose on to.

Home-video your party then play it back to the children just before home time. They'll love seeing themselves.

Organise all your running-around games before tea. You don't want children to be sick on those pretty party frocks!

For a culinary delight, sprinkle multi-coloured jelly babies into your jelly mixture before it sets.

If you are no good at making cakes, buy a bag of ready-made fairy cakes, arrange them on a plate in the shape of the birthday child's initial and place a candle on each cake. It saves mess, too, because each guest can have their own little cake.

If you don't have a big enough table for everyone, just put a plastic throwaway cloth on the floor and have a 'picnic' indoors.

To calm children down just before home time, try playing 'sleeping lions' or 'dead donkeys' (the children have to lie as still a possible; the winner is the one who moves the least).

'She was the archetypal mother: living only for her children, sheltering them from the consequences of their actions – and in the end doing them irreparable harm.' *Marcia Muller*

Use a wipe-clean board or blackboard at child eye-level near the phone for emergency numbers and numbers where you can be contacted if needed.

Stop children from getting into cupboards and drawers. Elastic bands make ideal safety catches. Just stretch them across adjacent doorknobs and the doors can only open a short distance.

Children have a habit of running into glass patio doors, thinking that they're open when they're not. Avoid a nasty accident by putting a few stickers on your glass doors.

Before storing carrier bags, tie them in a knot. It will then be much more difficult for a child to put one over his head without thinking.

To stop little fingers getting trapped in slamming doors, glue a small cork to the door frame so that the doors cannot actually slam shut.

Make windows safe for children. Instead of child bars, fix garden trellis across the bottom of the window.

If your house opens on to a busy road, a sensible precaution to take with toddlers about is to fix a baby gate across your porch or front doorway.

Put soft toys in the freezer once a month for at least six hours to kill dust mites, which can cause allergies. Once you take it out of the freezer, vacuum the toy to remove the mite faeces.

To plan a child's room, get down on the floor and view things from a child's perspective.

Brighten up a child's room by making fun borders. Get long strips of paper and let the children walk up and down them with painted feet.

Yes, your children can scribble on walls!
Just paint a section with matt black paint
and have a tub of chalks to hand.

Finally, enjoy your children. The early years
will go far too quickly.

'No matter how old a mother is, she
watches her middle-aged children for signs of
improvement.' *Florida Scott-Maxwell*

How It All Began

Mothering Sunday was also known as
Refreshment Sunday because the rules
governing fasting for Lent were relaxed on
that day. Simnel cake was traditionally
made for Mother's Day. It dates from around
the seventeenth century when young people
in service were given time off during Lent to
visit their families. Simnel cake is a fruit
cake with two layers of almond paste, one
on top and one in the middle. The cake is
made with 11 balls of marzipan icing on
top – some say they represent the 11 disci-
ples (Judas is not included) while others
believe that the 11 balls mark the months
of the year spent working away from home.
Traditionally, sugar violets would also be
added.

The name Simnel probably comes from the
Latin word *simila* which means a fine wheat
flour usually used for baking a cake. There's a
legend that a man called Simon and his wife
Nell argued over whether the Mothering

Sunday cake should be baked or boiled. In the end they did both, so the cake was named after both of them: SIM-NELL.

Simnel cake recipe

110 g/4 oz softened butter
110 g/4 oz soft brown sugar
110 g/4 oz self raising flour
3 eggs, beaten
12 oz mixed raisins, sultanas, currents (could also use dried apricots, cut into small pieces)
55 g/2 oz mixed peel
25 g/1 oz ground almonds
1 tsp mixed spice

For the marzipan (you can buy some or, if you're feeling Earth Mother-ish, make it yourself):

125 g/4 oz caster sugar
125 g/4 oz ground almonds
1 egg, beaten
1/2 tsp almond essence

To decorate:

Spring flowers such as violets and primroses
Egg white
Caster sugar

Method:

1 To make the marzipan, mix the sugar and ground almonds in a bowl. Add some of the beaten egg, enough to give a fairly soft consistency. Put the almond essence in and knead the mixture until it becomes a smooth paste. Roll out a third of the mixture into a circular shape, to fit a 7 in/18 cm cake tin. Reserve the rest of the marzipan for later.

2 Preheat the oven to 140°C/275°F/gas 2.

3 Put all the cake ingredients into a large bowl and gradually beat thoroughly until mixed together.

4 Put half the mixture into a greased and lined cake tin and place the rolled-out circle of marzipan on top. Spoon the rest of the cake mixture on top of this.

5 Bake in the oven for 1¹/₂ to 1³/₄ hours until the cake is golden brown and firm to the touch in the middle. If it looks like it's getting a bit too brown towards the end of the cooking time, cover it with foil.

6 Take the cake out of the oven and leave to cool before turning out on to a rack.

7 When the cake is cool, brush the top with the apricot jam. Roll out half of the remaining marzipan into a circle and place on top of the cake.

8 With the rest of the marzipan, make 11 even-sized balls and place on the edge of the cake.

9 Brush with beaten egg and glaze under a hot grill for a few minutes, turning the cake so that it browns evenly.

10 To prepare the flowers, put them on a rack. Whisk the egg white and then brush carefully over the petals.

11 Sprinkle caster sugar over so that it sticks to the flowers. Leave to dry and harden (an airing cupboard is ideal for this).

12 Remove the flowers from the rack and arrange on the cake.

Mother's Day is celebrated around the world but not at the same time and not everyone gets a bunch of flowers and some chocolates. In Norway, Mother's Day is on the second Sunday in February, while in Argentina, it's the second Sunday in October. Lebanon celebrates Mother's Day on the first day of spring, and in South Africa, it's the first Sunday in May.

In India, Hindus celebrate a 10-day festival called *Durga Puja* early in October, honouring Durga, the Divine Mother. Durga is supposed to be very tall with 10 arms. In each arm she carries a weapon to destroy evil.

Sweden also has a family holiday on the last Sunday in May. Shortly before Mother's Day the Swedish Red Cross sells tiny plastic flowers. The money from these 'Mother's Flowers' is used to give a holiday break to mothers with a lot of children.

In both Spain and Portugal, Mother's Day is closely linked to the church. The 8 December is the day that tribute is paid to the Virgin

Mary, Mother of Jesus. It is also the day when children honour their mothers.

In Serbia, they celebrate *Materice*, which takes place two weeks before Christmas. On *Materice* children creep into their mother's bedroom early in the morning and tie her up. Mother has to beg the children to untie her, promising to give them little gifts which she has (hopefully!) hidden under her pillow. Let's hope that's one tradition that doesn't catch on here!

Index